BRING HEAVEN DOWN TO EARTH

365 meditations

on the wisdom of the Rebbe,

Menachem Mendel Schneerson

condensed & compiled by Tzvi Freeman

Copyright © 1997, Tzvi Freeman. All rights reserved. This book or any part of it may not be reproduced without permission from the publisher; exceptions are made for brief excerpts in published reviews.

Eighth Edition

By the same author:

Bringing Heaven Down To Earth, Book II

Heaven Exposed

The Book of Purpose

Men, Women & Kabala

Trembling With Joy

Sales:

chasidusbooks@gmail.com

Permissions and comments:

info@theRebbe.com

For more of the same, visit:

www.chabad.org

Dedication

Many became leaders because we believed in them.

The Rebbe became a leader because he believed in us.

Putting this book together is my way

of not letting him down.

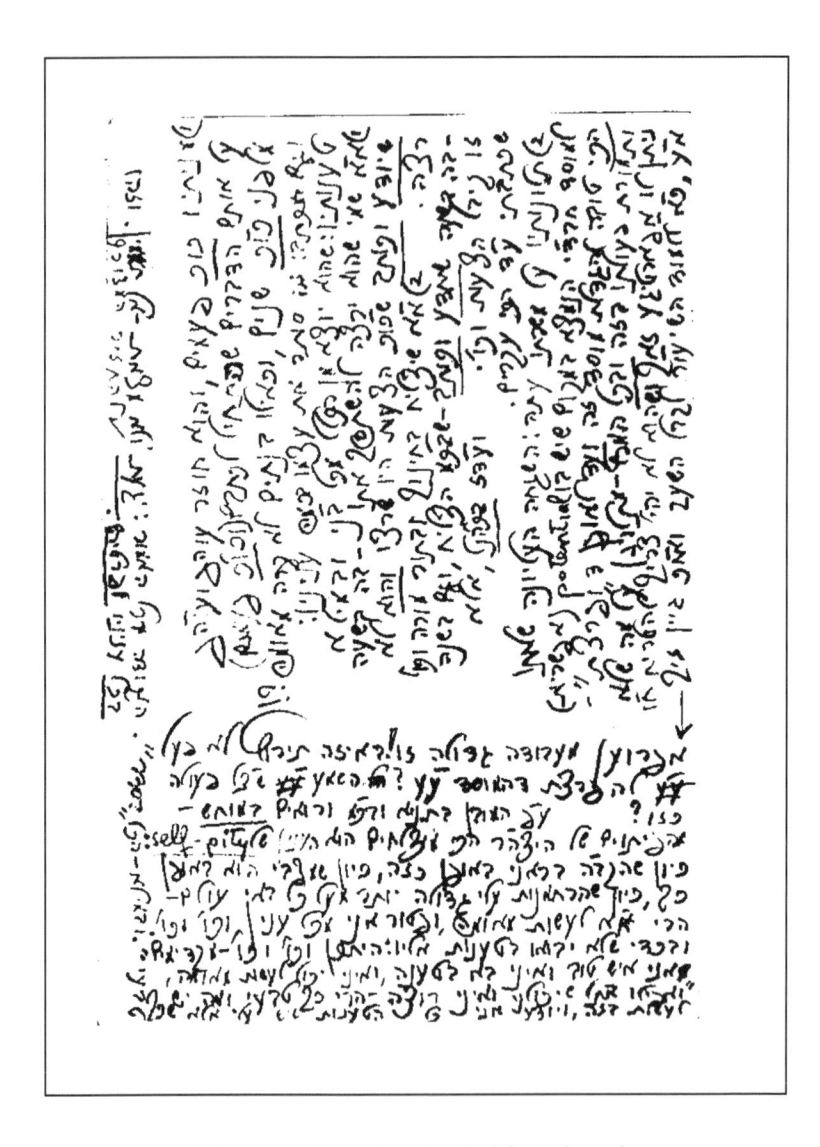

A letter written by the Rebbe's hand.

The letter is in Hebrew, with the exception of the words "potential" and "self-pity."

DON'T READ THIS BOOK

As a searching adolescent immersed in the thoughts of Lao Tse, Richard Alpert, the Dali Lama and Alan Watts, I still felt dissatisfaction—an empty craving left in my gut. It was not until I came across the teachings of the Rebbe that I felt that sense of, "these are the words of my heart speaking from within."

I went to study in the Rebbe's yeshivas for nine years, and continued learning for another ten while raising a family and making a living.

On the 3rd of Tammuz, 5754 (June 12, 1994), the Rebbe passed on. I felt a need to gather the pieces of everything the Rebbe had given me, to package them in tight little parcels so they shouldn't be lost. Then I put them in this book. When I look at the book I find the Rebbe still alive.

The Rebbe has been held prisoner in society's box of stereotype and preconception. People simply don't look in Brooklyn for modern day gurus. They are not searching out a rabbi in 18th century clothing. Perhaps had he hailed from the mountains of Tibet or taught psychoanalysis at Berkeley, perhaps…

But he never even tried to make himself marketable. He didn't dress it, he didn't speak it and he didn't seem to want it. So his light remained pure —but within.

This is how we'll liberate him, you and I:

Don't read this book. Live with it as I have. Make it a dialogue between the Rebbe and your life.

Take it little by little, day by day. When you need an answer, look here. When you need to come up for air, find it in the Rebbe's words. When life is getting tough and confusing, open up just anywhere—or choose a random number—and see what the Rebbe has to say.

If you find heaven, do us all a favor and bring it down to earth.

~

Some of the lines in this book are direct quotations translated from Yiddish or Hebrew. The bulk, however, are droplets condensed from a mass of teachings and concepts.

Sources include public talks, private correspondence, the Rebbe's personal diary and private notes, and some anecdotal material. Since everything the Rebbe taught is firmly grounded on the teachings of his predecessors, I have included vital legacy teachings that the Rebbe often cited.

~

A note about gender usage:

I use "…him" and "he will….", "a man" and all the other non-PC terms. The fact is, the Rebbe generally used the neutral Yiddish form of "one" as in "one will…." In Hebrew, the Rebbe was careful to use both the masculine and feminine form of "one will." English is terribly clumsy with these things, so I've committed the sins of mistranslation you read here.

CONTENTS

IN CONTEXT 9

FUSION 19

PURPOSE/ LIGHT 29

NATURE & THE MIRACULOUS 41

ALL THE WORLD IS MY TEACHER 55

MAKING A LIVING 67

STRUGGLE 85

FROM DESPAIR TO JOY 97

BRICK WALLS 109

COMING HOME 121

HEALING 129

BREAKING FREE 135

TRUTH 163

HIGHER LIFE 177

WE ARE ALL ONE 183

ACTS OF BEAUTY 199

BETWEEN WOMAN AND MAN 213

CHILDREN 223

ALL NOAH'S CHILDREN 227

THE BLUEPRINT OF CREATION 233

FAITH & INTELLECT 251

SCIENCE AND TECHNOLOGY 269

MY PEOPLE 275

DAYS ARE COMING… 283

TRANSMISSION 293

THE CREED OF NOAH 295

IN CONTEXT

No one rises above the earth by tugging at his own hairs. A prisoner cannot free himself from his prison. He needs first to bond with one who is already free.

And so, at an early age, I was looking for someone who could guide me—a mentor, a guru. But who will be your guide when you beat your own path?

My path has always been like those of the deer in the forest—skipping over, squeezing and breaking through, steering far from the clear highways that everyone else travels.

On my fifteenth birthday, I dropped out of high school. The year before I had been on the honor roll, and this year I was the grade ten president—but now I had no interest in following the established order.

When my parents made it clear that room and board were contingent upon my completing high school, I found a tutorial college that allowed me to take my exams that spring. And so, I found myself two years ahead of the game. Free—in my father's words—to associate with the fringe members of our society.

These were the early 70s in Vancouver—Canada's San Francisco. I gave classical guitar lessons and organized the "Anarchist Discussion Group" of the Vancouver Free University. I learned Tai Chi, Yoga, became a strict vegetarian, and attended countless "Encounter Groups." I hitchhiked around Canada, the U.S., Israel, Europe and the U.K. I found souls traveling and dabbling on every kind of path I never had imagined.

I returned with a broader mind, but still a craving, empty soul. None of what I found was for me. When you search, it doesn't matter where you look, the last thing you'll find is your own self.

I decided it was important to be able to do something well, and for me that would be music. I approached a well-known composer who lived in Vancouver for private lessons. She agreed, but after a few sessions, commanded one of her graduate students to take me by the hand and register me at the music college of the University of British Columbia. This was not the place I wanted to be, but I decided I would learn something. At the same time I began seriously practicing meditation, teaching Yoga, and became fascinated with Lao Tse.

Nevertheless, my soul's stomach was as empty as ever. Perhaps, I wondered, what I need is to go off and hide in a Zen monastery for a few years. The conflict of spirituality and sensuality, the metaphysical and the material career was ripping me apart. There was no real direction, only confusion. I remember praying with all my heart—not for any answers, not for any revelation—only that I should be able to talk heart to heart with my G‑d, because life in such a complicated, convoluted world makes it very hard to talk sincerely with your G‑d.

When a fish finds the ocean, it must dive in. When I first heard a talk of chassidic mysticism, it didn't matter that I had no comprehension of most of what was being said. Rain comes as a stranger to a land parched for generations by drought, but the earth remembers. What to my mind was foreign, to my guts was home.

That first splash of native waters came from a traveling student of the Rebbe. I recall how he explained to me that our purpose was to perceive the G-dliness within every created thing. From between his words, I perceived there was much more. At least a few thousand years of collective wisdom and beauty.

I wanted to know who taught this stuff. I wanted it explained to me. They told me there was a Rebbe in New York. "The Lubavitcher Rebbe."

~

"Rebbe" means a teacher. It is a term also used to refer to a master of the mystical path of Chassidic Judaism, as taught by the Baal Shem Tov.

"Lubavitch" refers to many things: A town in Byelorussia, a neighborhood in Brooklyn, and an international association.

Lubavitch, the town, was the seat of a line of Chassidic masters, rabbis who followed in the practical/mystical path of the Baal Shem Tov, as his teachings were elaborated by Rabbi Schneur Zalman of Liadi. At the outset of World War II, Lubavitch moved to Brooklyn.

"The Rebbe" is the title by which Rabbi Menachem Mendel Schneerson has come to be known worldwide.

Menachem Mendel Schneerson was born in 1902 to Rebbetzin Chana Schneerson and the kabalist and legalist, Rabbi Levi

Yitzchaak Schneerson, chief rabbi of Dniprepetrovs'k in the Ukraine. He studied at home, because the teacher at the Jewish school complained he had nothing to teach him.

In his teen years, his father gave him permission to study science, mathematics and languages—but with the warning, "G-d forbid any of this should take away from your sixteen hours a day of Torah study."

Young Menachem passed the government matriculation exams six months later. He also acquired a working knowledge of English, Italian, French, Gruzian and Latin.

Between the years 1928 to 1940, the Rebbe studied the sciences and humanities at the University of Berlin and at the Sorbonne in Paris. In 1941, he fled Nazi-occupied France for the U.S.A. For a short time he was employed as an engineer with the U.S. Navy. His work was labeled as "classified."

When the previous rebbe of Lubavitch passed away in 1950, the surviving remnants of Lubavitchers around the world turned immediately to his son-in-law, Rabbi Menachem Mendel Schneerson. Although he hid himself by dressing in modern clothes and avoiding any sort of prestige, they knew him as a great scholar and leader.

He was begged to take the leadership. He refused, repeatedly. He claimed he knew himself too well to imagine he might be fit for the job. When a delegation of elders came with a petition accepting Rabbi Schneerson as their Rebbe, he placed his head in his hands and began to cry. "Please, leave me alone," he pleaded. "This has nothing to do with me."

It was only after one complete year of such episodes the Rebbe finally accepted the position. Even then, it was with a condition: "I will help," the Rebbe announced, "But each of you must carry out your own mission. Don't expect to hang on to the fringes of my prayer shawl."

For the next 42 years, the Rebbe never missed a day at his office. Seven days a week, 365 days a year.

~

My first reaction was inspiration. I had to find out more about this man. After that, friends, relatives and acquaintances began to cool me off. They told me this was idol worship. They told me I was surrendering my power of thought and independence.

My intellect had to concur. Where was all my background in anarchist philosophy? After all, these were the reasons I had failed to follow any other guru or mentor more than a few steps. I did not want my mind taken away. I wanted my own path. I did not want to be swallowed alive by a larger ego.

That conflict continued for many years. There are some things you know inside, but the ego and all your rationalization refuses to allow that inner knowledge to take charge.

Nevertheless, today I find myself a chassid of the Rebbe and still my own self. The Rebbe just never matched the ego-consuming demagogue I had so much feared.

For one thing, the trappings were always conspicuously absent. No majestic, flowing robes. No magnificent estate. No private jet. A modest home in good taste and a bare bones office. Nothing on the outside to distinguish him from any of his chassidim.

He didn't need the big show. There was no ego involved. The Rebbe was a master of simplicity, at being nothing and just allowing the essential G-dliness of the soul to shine through. And so, he was able to guide others without consuming them.

As for my rebellious spirit, in the Rebbe I found the ultimate rebel. I could even say, you don't submit to the Rebbe—you rebel with him. It's a long tradition of the rebbes of Lubavitch to defy the monster the world feigns to be, to follow an inner vision, rather than the superficial perception of the flesh eyes. It is no surprise that every one of the Rebbe's predecessors spent time in czarist or communist prison. The Rebbe himself was forced into hiding before leaving Russia.

The Rebbe was an orthodox rebel, a traditional radical. In the sixties, the rest of the Jewish Establishment looked on in disdain at what was happening to their youth and cried, "Student unrest! Hippies and Freaks! This is certainly a deranged and lost generation."

The Rebbe declared, "Finally the iceberg of America is beginning to melt! Finally, its young people realize they do not have to conform!"

The Rebbe told his students to go out and bring Jewish youth in touch with their roots. He was ridiculed for it for years. Only after the strategy began to work did those who had mocked him jump on the bandwagon as well.

He was always a maverick, not consulting with others on his strategies and campaigns, often ridiculed for what they considered outrageous decisions. There were never any followers of the Rebbe—followers couldn't keep up. The Rebbe has only leaders. Those who rebel with him.

Perhaps most controversial—and least understood—was his vision of a new era dawning upon the world. Almost uniquely, the Rebbe mixed messianic vision with a down to earth embracement of the here-and-now. There were others in the past who shouted, "The Messiah is coming! Sell your homes and leave to the Holy Land!" The Rebbe shouted, "A new time is on its way! Build homes! Build institutions! Find meaning in all that is today. Be in that new time now."

～

Simchat Torah is a festive Jewish holiday. Every year at this time, the Rebbe's place of worship, 770 Eastern Parkway, Brooklyn, NY, packs in thousands of chassidim and all sorts of Jews celebrating with the Torah scrolls throughout the night, singing and dancing.

On Simchat Torah, 1977, amidst the festivities, the Rebbe turned pale. Suddenly, he turned from his place, walked through the entire hall, up the stairs, into his office and locked the door behind him. Only after much pleading, were they able to persuade him to unlock the door.

It became apparent that the Rebbe had suffered a heart attack. Typically, he had not wanted to disturb the festive mood.

The best doctors were immediately called. They had to come to the Rebbe, because the Rebbe refused to leave his office.

When the Rebbe asked what the people were doing in the synagogue downstairs, he was told they were crying and praying. He made a request: "Tell them the more they sing and dance, the better I will feel."

The chassidim danced and sang through the night like they never had before.

The Rebbe spent several weeks in his office under the doctors' care. It was noted that the healthiest activity for the Rebbe's heart was to study. The harshest activity was to read the letters that came to him. Many of the letters were from people in distress asking for blessing and advice. The Rebbe's heart would pulsate erratically in empathy for their sorrows.

When the doctors attempted to stop the delivery of letters to the Rebbe, the Rebbe intervened.

"You are trying to take away my livelihood," he protested.

For many years, the Rebbe granted private audiences three nights a week. Just about every kind of person you could imagine—activists, businessmen, scientists, politicians, journalists—waited their turn until two, three— occasionally even nine o' clock in the morning. The Rebbe talked warmly with each one, providing guidance and advice when solicited, blessings whether solicited or not.

Letters came from everywhere. Bags of letters, daily. But the Rebbe wouldn't allow anyone else to open letters to him. He read each one and instructed his personal secretary, Dr. Mindel, what to write back—and then edited after him. Much of this book is derived from those letters.

But the central fountain from which we drank in the Rebbe's wisdom was the "farbrengen." This was when we all packed tightly together as the Rebbe spoke for timeless hours, filling the interludes with song and l'chaim. Those who came with questions left with answers and those who came knowing all the answers left understanding just how much there is to ask. The Rebbe's words were broadcast live over a network of telephone lines—and later, by satellite—to listeners all over the globe and then transcribed into print, often to be heavily edited by the Rebbe's hand.

In 1983, on the occasion of his 80th birthday, U.S. Congress proclaimed the Rebbe's birthday, "Education Day U.S.A." and awarded him the National Scroll of Honor. In 1995, the Rebbe was (posthumously) awarded the Congressional Gold Medal, an award granted only 130 Americans since Thomas Jefferson, for "outstanding and lasting contributions."

My editor says I must add something about his passing. But for me he has never passed on, nor has he for any of his true students. For us, as for him, his life was never the physical body. It was his words, his wisdom, his spirit that we felt inside us. And that is all still here with us, as vibrant as the day we heard from his mouth. If enough people will read this book and recognize what great wisdom lived amongst them, he will be even more alive than ever before.

A well-known author came for a private audience with the Rebbe. After he left the Rebbe's office, he turned to the chassidim, and accused them, "You are thieves! You are stealing from the entire world! You have taken the Rebbe and made him exclusively your own, as though he were a Rebbe just for you Lubavitchers."

"But the Rebbe is the Rebbe of the entire world!"

Let us liberate him, you and I.

—*Tzvi Freeman, Tammuz 5757, Vancouver*

FUSION

The teachings of the Rebbe are not just a collection of advice and nice thoughts—just as a year is more than the sum of 365 days. The teachings of the Rebbe make up one simple whole. All revolve around the same essential concept: The fusion of the loftiest spiritual heights with the most mundane physicality. In the Rebbe's words, "the highest with the lowest."

The concept is not only radical but powerful: It means I can be myself, living a "down to earth" existence, and yet fulfilling a transcendental goal. It means that there is nothing we are trying to escape—other than the notion that we must escape something. We don't run away from this world to join a higher one, instead we work to fuse the two. We aren't in the business of "making it to heaven"—we're busy bringing heaven down to earth.

1) Down To Earth

When it all began, Heaven was here on Earth.

The physical plane, more than any of the higher spiritual worlds, was the place where the Divine Presence yearned to be.

But Man, step by step, banished the Divine Presence from its home, with a tree of knowledge, with a man who murdered his brother, with all those things
that human beings do…

Since Man chased it away, only Man can bring it back. And this began with Abraham, who proclaimed Oneness for all the world.

And it ends with us.
Our generation will bring Heaven back down to Earth.

2) Us

Each generation has its role in history.

From all the generations before us we inherited a wealth of dreams: philosophy, truths, wisdom and purpose. We are tiny midgets standing on the shoulders of their ideas and their noble deeds.

Our generation's mandate—and destiny—
is to make the dream real.

3) Home

Those who study the Kabbalah understand that there are infinite worlds beyond ours and beyond the worlds of the angels, all filled with divine light, beauty and oneness.

But know also that all these are but a means to an end;
all were brought into being with a single purpose:
G-d desires to be at home within your mundane world.

4) The Bridge

Animals do not gaze at the stars and angels are confined to the realm of the spirit, but Man is G-d's bridge between heaven and earth.

Our bodies are formed from the dust, our souls are of the essence of G-d. We alone can look at a physical world and see spiritual life and beauty. We who are beyond both heaven and earth, form and matter, spirit and body —we alone can fuse the two.

5) Seeing Within

Man sees a tree and the tree says, "I am here, I was here, and I am nothing more but a thing that is here."

Man ponders and answers, "No! I give you a name! You are "tree"! You have beauty and you have a soul. You point upwards and you say, "There is something higher, there is the One who gives me life and gives me my very being."

And so Man goes on, until he has brought the whole of creation down upon its knees.

Man alone can accomplish what the angels cannot. Man alone can discover the spiritual within the material.

6) G-d's Plea

They have banished G-d into exile.

They have decreed He is too holy, too transcendent to belong in our world.

They have determined He does not belong within the ordinary, in the daily run of things.

And so they have driven Him out of His garden, to the realm of prayer and meditation, to the sanctuaries and the secluded places of hermits.

They have sentenced the Creator to exile and His creation they have locked in a dark, cold prison.

And He pleads, "Let me come back to my garden, to the place in which I found delight when it all began."

7) Essence Garden

There are people who do much good, but with pessimism—because to them the world is an inherently bad place. They do good things, but without light and vitality. Who knows how long it can last?

We must know that this world is not a dark, sinister jungle, but a garden. And not just any garden, but G-d's own pleasure garden, full of beauty, wonderful fruits and fragrances, a place where G-d desires to be with all His essence.

If the taste to us is bitter, it is only because we must first peel away the outer shell to find the fruit inside.

8) Higher Lower

The higher something is, the lower it falls. So too, the loftiest revelations are to be found in the lowest places.

Therefore, if you find yourself in a place seemingly devoid of anything spiritual—don't despair. The lower you are, the higher you can reach.

9) Bigger Than Big

G-d is not just *big*—He is infinite.

If He were only *big,* then those things that are small would be further from Him and those things that are big would be closer. But to the Infinite, big and small are irrelevant terms. He is everywhere
and He is found wherever He wishes to be found.

10) Microhealing

Every person is a microcosm of the entire Creation. When a person brings harmony between his G-dly soul and his material life, he brings harmony between the whole of heaven and earth.

11) A Story

A favorite story of the Rebbe, central to his activist view of life:

Rabbi Schneur Zalman of Liadi, the first rebbe of the Lubavitch dynasty, led the services for Yom Kippur, the holiest day of the year. He stood wrapped in his prayer shawl, profoundly entranced in the cleaving of the soul to its source. Every word of prayer he uttered was fire. His melody and fervor carried the entire community off to the highest and the deepest journey of the spirit.

And then he stopped. He turned, cast off his prayer shawl and left the synagogue. With a bewildered congregation chasing behind, he walked briskly to the outskirts of town, to a small dark house from where was heard the cry of a newborn infant. The rabbi entered the house, chopped some wood and lit a fire in the oven, boiled some soup and cared for the mother and child that lay helpless in bed.

Then he returned to the synagogue and to the ecstasy of his prayer.

…

The Rebbe added:

Note that the rabbi removed his prayer shawl. To help someone, you must leave your world, no matter how serene, to enter the place where that person lives.

12) Return to One

In the ancient Book of Formation, it is written, "If your heart races, return to One."

There are times when you find yourself in a state of inspiration, uplifted from the banalities of everyday life. At this time you must "return to One"—to the oneness of heaven and earth: You must resolve how this heavenly state will affect your earthly life.

13) On the Third Day There Was Peace

First there was One. There was no peace, because there was nothing with which to make peace. There was only One.

Then there was Two. There was Plurality. From this point on, an infinite cacophony of conflict extended in all directions and forever.

And on the third day G-d created peace.

Peace is not homogeneity. Peace does not mean that everyone thinks the same way. Peace is when there is plurality that finds a higher Oneness.

14) Essential Peace

There are three ways to bring unity between two opposites:

The first is by introducing a power that transcends both of them and to which they both utterly surrender their entire being. They are then at peace with each other because they are both under the influence of the same force. But their *being* is not at peace—their *being* is simply ignored.

The second way is by finding a middle ground where the two beings meet. The two are at peace where they meet on that middle ground—but the rest of their territory remains apart and distant.

The third way is to reveal that the essence of every aspect of the two beings is one and the same.

PURPOSE/ LIGHT

There is a recurring theme in the volumes of stories told of the Rebbe: The tale of the man who was in the right place at the right time.

There are the stories of someone embarking on a trip to some distant place, and the Rebbe gave him a book to take along, or asked him to do a certain thing there, or to meet a certain person. Or the Rebbe simply asked someone to go to a place, with little direction of what to do there.

And then, in these stories, it always works out that just at the right time the right person turns up in the right place and the entire story unfolds.

It's all a matter of making connections: Every soul has certain sparks of light scattered throughout the world that relate to it in particular. The Rebbe sees the soul and senses, like a Geiger counter, the sparks that await this soul. All that was needed is to bring the two within a reasonable proximity and the rest takes care of itself.

The stories are meant as a teaching as well. The Rebbe was revealing to us the wonder of our own lives, that there is purpose latent in whatever you are doing.

15) Become Light

The mandate of the whole of Creation is stated almost immediately: They translate it as "Let their be light." But instead, read, "It should become Light."

Meaning that the entire world—even the darkness—should become a source of light and wisdom.

16) Refilling the Void

It all began with an infinite light that filled all and left no room for a world to be. Then that light was withheld so the world might be created in the resulting void.

Then the world was created,
with the purpose of returning to that original state of light
—yet to remain a world.

17) Light Unsheathed

All the world's problems stem from light being withheld.

Our job then, is to correct this. Wherever we find light, we must rip away its casings, exposing it to all, letting it shine forth to the darkest ends of the earth.

Especially the light you yourself hold.

18) Functional Light

G-d did not give you light for you to
hold it up in the middle of the day.

When you are given light it is in order to *accomplish*
something, to do something difficult and novel.

Go take your light and transform the darkness
and it will also shine!

19) Stay Put

When you come to a place that seems
outside of G-d's realm, too coarse for light to enter,
and you want to run away…

…know that there is no place outside of G-d,
and rejoice in your task of uncovering Him there.

20) More Light

Fighting evil is a very noble activity when it must be done.

But it is not our mission in life.

Our job is to bring in more light.

21) Every Detail

The Rebbe describes the following
as a central teaching of the Baal Shem Tov:

Not only the pirouettes of a leaf as it falls off a tree,
the quivering of a blade of grass in the wind,
each and every detail of existence
brought into being, given life
and directed every moment from Above

—but beyond that:
every nuance is an essential component
of a grand and G-dly scheme,
the gestalt of all those vital minutiae.

Every moment burns with the pulse of G-d's desire.

Meditate on this. And then think:
How much more so the details of my daily life.

22) Now

For hundreds of years,
perhaps since the beginning of Creation,
a piece of the world has been waiting for your soul
to purify and repair it.

And your soul,
from the time it was first emanated and conceived, waited
above to descend to this world
and carry out that mission.

And your footsteps were guided to reach that place.

And you are there now.

23) 42 Journeys

The Baal Shem Tov taught that each of our lives is comprised of 42 journeys, corresponding to the 42 journeys of the Children of Israel in the wilderness.

Some of those journeys have pleasant names. Others don't sound so nice. But none are inherently bad. It is only that you may have to dig deeper and deeper to find the purpose and the good within them.

24) Be There

In each journey of your life you must *be* where you are.
You may only be passing through on your way to somewhere else seemingly more important—nevertheless,
there is purpose in where you are
right now.

25) Each Day

Purify time.

Each day, find an act of kindness and beauty

that belongs to that day alone.

26) The Moment

Every moment has two faces:

It is a moment defined by the past from which it extends and by the future to which it leads.

And it is a moment for itself,

with its own meaning, purpose and life.

27) Your Jerusalem

People want to run away from where they are, to go to find
their Jerusalem—as if elsewhere they will find perfection.
Wherever you are, whatever you are doing there,
make *that* a Jerusalem.

28) Running Away

When you run from the responsibility of one place to be in
another, two things are amiss:
The place where you are needed,
and the place where you are and shouldn't be.

29) Just a Favor

The Baal Shem Tov taught that a soul may descend from its place high in the heavens into this world for 70–80 years, just to do a favor for another.

30) Perceptive Repair

If you see what needs to be repaired and how to repair it, then you have found a piece of the world that G-d has left for you to complete.
But if you only see what is wrong and how ugly it is, then it is yourself that needs repair.

NATURE & THE MIRACULOUS

There is a thread, a chain of souls with a common mission, each one completing what the other left undone.

Seven generations back, 200 years ago, lived the first Schneerson, Rabbi Schneur Zalman of Liadi. Schneur Zalman was a great philosopher with the unique ability to draw into the words of intellect that which others could only feel deep in the soul. So he wrote a short book—a classic now known as "The Tanya"—in which he explained how there is nothing but G‑d.

He explained that every detail of existence is constantly created at every moment, each detail by a particular force of G‑d invested within it. He asserted that if the power of existence would be removed, that thing would cease to exist. In fact, it would never have existed—its past would also cease, since time, too, is a creation.

Which means that everything that happens comes from Above. Which means that G‑d can be found anywhere, at any time, in any thing and by anybody. Which means that splitting the Red Sea or stopping the sun in its path are minor miracles when compared to the very fact that we all continue to exist. Because every moment we are all created anew, something from nothing.

Eventually, even the students of opposing teachings accepted his views, which swiftly became mainstream thought. The ideas found their way into secular thought as well. Today, few realize from where the idea of constant creation came.

So, when the Rebbe expressed these same thoughts, and applied them to modern life, he came by them honestly. They were in his blood.

31) World Defined

Where G-d is hidden—there you see a world.

32) Higher Reality

We take the laws of nature too seriously. We think of the world as though it exists just as its Creator exists.

Therefore, we must have miracles.

A miracle is a state of enlightenment that says, "Our reality is nothing but a glimmer of a Higher Reality. In that Higher Truth, there is no world. There is nothing else but Him."

33) Imagining

Meditate upon the ray of light that pierces through a window on a sunny day—and imagine how that ray exists engulfed within its source, the sun. So too, are the cosmos a nothingness absorbed within their Source, the Infinite Light.

Imagine the entire universe as a stream of conscious thought, and imagine how a single thought exists in its place of birth, a place before words, before things, where there is only One.

We created beings cannot perceive the Source with our flesh eyes, and so we see a world.

But to the Source, there is no being, no entity, only the Infinite Light.

34) G-d Involved

When a parent loves a child,

He stoops down to the child, with such love, he leaves his language to speak the language of the child, he leaves his place to play the games of the child, he leaves his entire world and all the maturity he has gained in thirty, forty years or more to become excited, sincerely excited, by those things that excite the child, to react as the child reacts, to *live* with the child in the child's world with all his being…

But he is not a child. He is an adult, even as he plays with the child. Precisely *because* he is *truly* an adult, he can allow himself to be a child and remain an adult.

G-d feels our pain and our joy. He lives intimately with us in our world. Yet He is infinite, beyond all things—even as He is here with us.

35) Not and Is

G-d is not Nature.

But Nature is G-dly.

36) Recognition

When G-d makes a miracle, it is so that afterwards we may look at the natural order of things and say,
"I recognize this. This is not what it appears to be.
This, too, is a miracle."

37) Peek-A-Boo

Everywhere in the world, parents play peek-a-boo with their children.

It is a major discovery of life, a cornerstone in human development: to realize that something is there even when you cannot see it, that the world is not defined by your subjective perception, that there is something that absolutely *is*—whether you know of it or not.

All our life, all of the world, is G-d playing with us that same game. He peeks with a miracle and then hides behind nature.

Eventually, we look behind nature to find Him there.

38) Impossible

G-d can do anything. He could even, as the saying goes, "fit an elephant through the eye of a needle."

So, how would He do it? Would He make the elephant smaller? Or would He expand the eye of the needle?

Neither. The elephant would remain big, the eye of the needle small. And He would fit the elephant through the eye of the needle.

Illogical? True. But logic is just another of His creations. He who created logic is permitted to disregard it.

39) Stereo Lighting

When the world was made, G-d was left with two lights: A light of boundless energy that encompasses all things and gives them being, but transcends them, and a penetrating light that vitalizes all things but is limited and darkened by them.

The first light is a pure expression of "there is none else but He," so from it extend miracles, acts that deny the world any significance.

The second light is an expression of His desire that there be a world, so from it extends the natural order of things, a world of elements behaving as though they are directed by their own properties.

But G-d did not want a world where there are two Powers-That-Be—one of Nature and one of Supernature. So He made the two lights to play in harmony, quietly divulging to those who wish to know that they both shine from a single Source.

How does He do it? Does He blunt the miracles so they could fit into the natural order? Or does He alter the properties of nature to compromise with the miracles?

Neither. Each element acts according to its natural properties, while miracles of the highest order occur.

Impossible? Plant a seed and watch it grow. Plant good deeds and watch with wonder the miracles that ensue.

40) Stereo-Miracles

There are two types of miracles: Those beyond nature and those clothed within it. The water of the Nile turning into blood was beyond nature. The victory of the Maccabees over the Greek army cam dressed as a natural occurrence—they had to fight to win.

Both types of miracles are necessary.

If we would only see miracles *beyond* nature, we would know that G-d can do whatever He likes—but we might think He must break the rules to do so. We would know a G-d who is beyond nature, but not within it.

If we would see only miracles that are *invested within* nature, we would know a G-d that is Master of all that happens within nature.
But we might think He is limited within it.

Now we know a G-d that is at once both beyond all things and within them.

In truth, there is nothing else but Him.

41) The Most Wondrous

There are open miracles that break the laws of
nature as though they were meaningless
—miracles any fool can perceive.

Then there are miracles that take some thought to realize,
that, yes, something out of the ordinary occurred here.

And then there are miracles so great, so wondrous, that no
one but G-d Himself is cognizant of them.

They are the miracles that occur continuously,
at every moment.

42) Determinism

The world is not predictable. Determinism is a leftover artifact of the nineteenth century. All we can say is that there are some loose rules by which G-d generally plays.

43) Miracles Today

In the year 1991:

The fall of the communist dictatorships of the Eastern Bloc was a kind of miracle that has no historical precedent. Never before were so many people affected by such radical change with so little violence.

The miracles of the Gulf War were open miracles. The same scud missiles that took countless lives in Iran were impotent when they struck their target in Israel. The soldiers and officers of the Allied Forces saw inexplicable miracles in their victory. Other miracles took some thought to realize that they were miracles, that the laws of nature were not the only thing at play here. But anyone who saw what occurred in the Gulf War saw openly that this was miraculous.

And yet people ask, "Where are the miracles today?"

44) The Inexplicable

To a fool, that which cannot be explained cannot exist.

The wise man knows that existence itself
cannot be explained.

45) Be a Miracle

Lead a supernatural life and G-d will provide the miracles.

ALL THE WORLD IS MY TEACHER

The Rebbe would sit down with his students and say, time and time again:

The Baal Shem Tov taught that from every thing a person hears or sees in this world he must find a teaching in how Man should serve G-d. In truth, this is the whole meaning of service of G-d.

46) Nuclear Lessons

Even from the most horrible things we can learn great lessons. From the threat of nuclear destruction we can learn several things about how to rearrange the
world for the good:

You don't need great armies.

It can take only one simple act.

You don't have to understand how it works
—just what button to press.

It doesn't matter who does it
—as long as he presses the right button.

From the smallest things come the biggest changes.

Tremendous power has always been there
—it needs only be revealed.

…and since all this has only been discovered in our generation, it must be of particular relevance to us.

47) Momentous Missions

Take-off of one of the Apollo missions was delayed due to a single, tiny loose component. From this the Rebbe learned:

The more momentous the mission,
the more crucial the details.
Including the most momentous mission of all,
the purpose of Creation.

Every detail of G-d's world and of our mission upon it
is essential. Nothing is without meaning.
Nothing is without vital purpose.

48) The Astronaut

A thought from a student of the Rebbe, Dr. Velvl Greene—a thought the Rebbe much appreciated.

You are an astronaut, far beyond the earth on a very long journey. Let's say you get fed up with the constant barrage of instructions coming in on your radio from home base. So you shut it off. With no regrets. And you relax, enjoying the awesome scenery out the window. And time flies by…

But eventually, you realize you have no clue where you are. Or how to get back to where you want to be. And you remember that you had a mission, but you can't quite get straight exactly what it was. You panic.

Finally, you remember the radio. You reactivate it. You hold the hand piece and call, "Home base? Astronaut calling home base! Answer me!!"

A faint reply is heard. It is the sweetest sound you've ever come by. Now you can get back on course.

Humankind, too, was given a mission.

49) Howard Hughes

He felt he could trust no one, for they were all only after his money. For the last twenty years of his life he could only hide from the entire world, without a friend, without any sort of enjoyment of life.

There was a man who had everything, and everything he had was a chain around his neck.

He was like all of us. We hold the keys to our freedom, but we use them to lock ourselves in.

50) On Computers

Told in the days of the Big Computer to my father-in-law, Avraham Polichenco, professor of computer science:

What is new about the computer? You walk into a room and you see familiar machines: A typewriter, a tape recorder, a television, a telephone, audio speakers, of course a calculator—but none of these are new.

Unseen, however, beneath the floors and behind the walls, are cables connecting these machines to work together as one. A digital technology allows them to all speak the same language—thereby transforming them from many ordinary machines into a single powerful computer.

Now, let's take your own life. You do business, you study, you eat, you talk—each activity seemingly irrelevant to the next. A mess of fragments.

And such, too, is the native psyche of the human being: We have minds that understand one way, hearts that feels another—and what we do has often nothing to do with either of those.

Apply the technology of the computer and in terms of your everyday life: Find a common meaning at which all these fragments converge, and thereby unleash their power.

51) One Candle at a Time

On the first night of Chanukah, all eight candleholders stand before you. But you light only one. Tomorrow night you shall light two. You know that eventually you will light all eight.

From which we learn two things:

First:
Move step by step in life.
Take things on at a pace you can handle.

Second:
Always grow. Always keep moving. If you did one good thing yesterday, do two today. Your ultimate achievement is always one step ahead.

52) Birthdays

Why do you celebrate your birthday?

In your mother's womb, you were comfortable, warm and cared for.

Then, you left. It was an ordeal, a trauma. The world you entered was cold and harsh. The mere act of living became a struggle. You cried.

Yet, every year you celebrate that day.

Because the day you were born was the day you became your own entity. No longer an extension of someone else. A proactive force in the world.

So, celebrate your birthday. And take time to think:
What have *I* given the world that was *not* given to me?
Was I really born?

53) Laser Power

People have the wrong idea about restrictions: They imagine that if you restrict what you eat and what you do not, when you work and when you meditate and pray, what you wear, where you go—all these restrictions will suffocate any sense of inspiration.

The truth is, without any restrictions your inspiration will quickly dissipate. Focus your light like a laser into an intense, powerful beam and it will last.

54) Electricity

Electricity helps us understand the hidden force within Creation:
It cannot be grasped with any of the five senses—we can only know it from its effects and causations. Yet from it we derive great light and power.

55) Beauty

Beauty cannot be touched.

It cannot be described of explained.

The more we uncover Beauty, the more it eludes us.

Beauty is where the world makes a window
through which the light of the Infinite can shine.

56) Black Holes

In recent years, astronomers have discovered that not all stars shine. There are some stars of such tremendous density, instead of radiating outwards they only draw light in. Therefore, they have named these stars, "Black Holes."

Fortunately, the universe has enough Black Holes already. If you have light, shine forth.

57) Sunglasses

The body is not something to be abhorred or rejected. On the contrary, the body serves as sunglasses for the soul.

Without the body, the soul can only perceive G-dliness in an abstract, ethereal way.

The body allows the soul to stare straight into the face of G-dliness, in tangible, concrete terms.

58) Metaphor

Everything we see about us is but a reflection of that which is above.

A king in our world is a reflection of the concept of Kingship above.

The sweetness of a fruit is a reflection of the sweetness of the Supernal Wisdom.

The form of the human body reflects the inner structure of the cosmos, so that each limb and organ parallels a particular Divine force.

Each of these things descends from its G-dly place into our material realm to take tangible form—so that we can grasp those G-dly concepts from which they extend.

Even those inventions that only arose in the modern era were in fact hidden all this time within the Creation, waiting for us to discover them and reconnect them with their G-dly source and meaning.

MAKING A LIVING

After the Rebbe suffered a severe heart attack in his 75th year, he came back up from the depths holding brilliant new jewels of enlightenment. Wondrously, the jewels were not couched in the settings of the Rebbe's immediate world—a world of study, meditation and prayer—but in the story of one who struggles to retain spirituality while squeezing the world for a paycheck.

Those who had taken career advice from the Rebbe now realized how intimately he lived with them in their struggle.

When the world was made the most blinding sparks of light fell to the lowest places. So there, in the super-fragmented world of money and eking out a living, there the Rebbe sees no dichotomy, nothing separate from G-d—only a grand purpose, a great mine in which to discover divine jewels of such value, they have never seen the light of day.

59) Unlimited Channels

You have today's meal before you on the table
and you sit and fret over what will be tomorrow
—and you claim you are "just being practical"!
This is not being practical—this is being confused.

Every day you are nourished straight from His full, open and overflowing hand. Everything in between—all your work and accounts and bills and receivables and clientele and prospects and investments—all is but a cloud of interface between His giving hand and your soul, an interface of no real substance that He bends and flexes at whim.

If so, if He is feeding you today, and He has fed you and provided all you need and more all these days, what concerns could you have about tomorrow? Is there then something that could stand in His way? Could He possibly have run out of means to provide for you?

Take your focus off the measured channels by which you receive and place your eyes on the Infinite Source of Giving. The Source has no lack of channels.

60) Attitude

The reason you have a business is to reconnect all these fragments back to their Creator. And the gauge of your success is your attitude.

If you see yourself as a victim of circumstance, of competitors, markets and trends, that your bread is in the hands of flesh and blood…

…then your world is still something separate from your G-d.

But if you have the confidence that He is always with you in whatever you do and the only one who has the power to change your destiny is you yourself through your own acts of goodness…

…then your earth is tied to the heavens.

And since in the heavens nothing is lacking,
so too it shall be in your world.

61) Not Making a Living

The common conception of how the system works is faulty.

They see a career as *making a living*. A career doesn't *make* anything. What you receive is generated above, in a spiritual realm.

Your business is to set up a channel to allow all that to flow into the material world.

62) Tailored to Business

Every business is the business of a tailor: to make clothes for the blessings that come your way.

You can't alter the size of your blessings by putting them in bigger clothes—on the contrary, they might just be chased away.

But neither must the clothes be too short.

Because that is the whole purpose: that miracles and blessings should not come into the world stark naked, but be clothed in the natural world.

And we are the tailors.

63) Joseph

Joseph was imprisoned in Egypt. He knew there was purpose in his being there; that when the time came he would be released.

Eventually, it happened: Pharaoh's cupbearer asked Joseph to interpret his dream. Joseph thought, "This is it! This man is the means by which I shall be redeemed."

He interpreted the dream favorably: the cupbearer would soon be released. And he asked one thing: "Plead for me before Pharaoh."

The dream was fulfilled; the cupbearer was released.
And he promptly forgot Joseph until two years later.

The wise men say that had Joseph not relied on the Egyptian, but solely on G-d alone, he would have been released two years earlier.

There is no person, no thing, no scheme upon which your livelihood or your fate rests.
There is only the flow of blessing from Above.

True, that flow clothes itself in tangible means, in job opportunities, in new clientele, in fresh markets, in well-connected acquaintances
—but all these are only channels, not the source. Grasp any one of them and it may crumble in your hands.

Grasp the Source of Life.

64) Do

If you are an upright person then, "G-d will bless you in everything you do." Note, however, it says you must *do*.

We are meant to work through the processes of the material world. Why? Because this is the means by which the world is enlightened: the spiritual must invest itself into the mundane. And this can only be achieved by spiritual people working within the everyday world.

65) Anxiety

Working for a living is good. It's the *anxiety* over making a living that is not good.

Don't let your inner self get involved in your business. That inner self must be preserved for fulfilling your purpose in life. Making lots of money is not your purpose in life.

66) The Ark

There is a raging storm at sea. There are hellish waves that crash and pound at the shore, carrying all away, leaving desolation behind.

The sea is the world of making a living. The waves are the stress and anxiety of indecision, not knowing which way to turn, on what to rely. Up and down, hot and cold—constantly churning back and forth.

Do as Noah did and build an ark.

An ark in Hebrew is "taiva"—which means also "a word." Your ark shall be the words of meditation and of prayer.

Enter into your ark, and rather than drown you with everything else, let the waters lift you up.

67) Mighty Waters

When the Mighty Waters cover your head, suffocating the soul and the flame that burnt inside…
When raging torrents of confusion drag you away in their current, ripping you from your hold on Life…
Look deeper. Beyond the soul.

For the soul itself, as well as the flame it holds, are rooted in a serene G-dly World of Emanation, a world of quietness and sublime harmony.

But the turbulence of this world is rooted even higher, in a World of Confusion, of light unbounded and untamed, before the orderly emanation of defined being,

> "—and the world was confused and void,
> with darkness over the face of the deep."

So you must dig deeper than those roots, to find the coals from which the flame arose and the flint rock from which the spark was struck. Deeper, until you reach the primordial essence of the soul, beyond Emanation, beyond Light—even beyond the unbounded light of pre-creation. Where there is nothing but the seminal thought that inspired all that is and was and will come to be.

And what was that thought?
It was the thought of you here and now, in your struggle with this world, and the delicious taste of your victory.

68) Who Will Win

Ultimately, the waters cannot drown the soul, but only lift it above them—for, in truth, this is the purpose for which they were created.

69) Toil

A meditation for when things get rough:

The world was brought into being with Goodness. And the ultimate good for a human being is that he should not be shamed, but feel as a partner in the fulfillment of the Divine Plan. Free bread is to us bread of shame—such is the nature of humankind.

That is why nothing good comes without toil. And according to the toil, can be known the harvest to be reaped.

70) Matching Worlds

Depression, anxiety and pessimism damage
the channels of blessing from Above.

The Zohar explains that there is a lower world—our world—and there is a higher world. Our world is meant to continuously receive from that higher world, but always according to our personal state of mind.

If we are glowing with joy and vitality, then that world shines upon us in its full glory.

But if it we wallow in depression and anxiety, then we can only receive a finely metered trickle of life squeezed through a constricted channel.

That is why King David said, "Serve G-d with joy!"
Because your joy here draws a higher joy from above.

71) Following Advice

There is no place for worry. You try to decide a course of action. If you do not have the experience to decide, you ask the advice of someone who does—a parent, a teacher, an expert—someone reliable, but also someone who is conscientious of your spiritual path.

Once you have decided what should be done, follow that course, confident that since you are doing what you believe in, the Master of All Things will support your decision.

72) Stay Calm

When things don't work out, relax.

Even if it's all your fault and you deserve everything you're getting, trust in G-d that it is all for the good, and stay calm.

When He sees how much you trust in Him,
He will make it for the good.

73) Believing in Good

There are two paths: One: Everything is *for* the good. Perhaps not immediately, but eventually good will come out from it.

The other: Everything *is* truly good—because there is nothing else but He Who is Good. It's just a matter of holding firm a little longer, unperturbed by the phantoms of our limited vision, unimpressed by the paper tiger that calls itself a world, and eventually we will be granted a heart to understand and eyes to see. Eventually, it will become obvious good in our world as well.

74) Unveiling the Spark

In every hardship, search for the spark of good and cling to it. If you cannot find that spark, rejoice that wonder beyond your comprehension has befallen you.

Once you have unveiled and liberated the spark of good, it can rise to overcome its guise of darkness and even transform the darkness fully to light.

75) Confidence

Trusting in the One Above doesn't mean waiting for miracles.

It means having confidence in what you are doing right now—because you know He has put you on the right path and will fill whatever you do with divine energy and blessing from on high.

76) Lofty Living

Realize that for you to make a living there must occur constant miracles. The fact that you may not notice these miracles doesn't make them any less wondrous.

On the contrary, it could be that they are so wondrous as to transcend your perception.

77) Harmony

A good barometer to determine whether something will be of benefit materially is whether it is the proper thing to do spiritually. A business venture that implies breaking your moral principles will also be detrimental materially.

At times, we experience tremendous pressure when our ethics seem to stand in the way of success—but this is only an illusion. The spiritual and the material are in conflict only to our subjective eyes. In fact, they work in harmony as one.

78) Getting Out of the Way

Sometimes you see that things have been taken out of your hands and are following a supernatural order. At this point, just do your best at what you have to do—and stay out of G-d's way.

79) Spiritual Career

Just as you search out a material career, so you must also search out a spiritual one.

But there is a difference:

With a material career you can only plow and sow and await the rains.

With your spiritual career you must provide the rain as well. It is up to you to fill your deeds with life.

80) Rather Be Praying

It's a paradox: The greatest revelations are to be found not in meditation, study and prayer, but in the mundane world—yet this is true only if you would rather be meditating, studying and praying.

81) Slaves of Stuff

There was a time when people did not have careers. People did not live to acquire material wealth.

People worked to earn enough for their families to eat that day, with a little extra saved for a special occasion. Today we are slaves of the houses, the cars and the gadgets we must acquire.

82) Priorities

The natural tendency is to treat matters of the spirit as luxury items—sort of an appendage to life.

Eating, sleeping, making money—these things are given priority and the time dedicated to them is sacrosanct.
But prayer, meditation and study fit in only when you feel like it, and are pushed aside on the slightest whim.

You've got to make your priorities faithful to your inner self. You've got to ask yourself if this is what your life is all about.

Set a schedule for spiritually enriching activities.
Be as tough with that schedule as a workaholic would be with his business.

83) The Choice

In truth, there are two possible channels from which to choose. It all depends on the perspective you take in life:

You could decide to become just another element of nature, chasing through the chaos after your bread, running the race of survival of the fittest.

You might even prosper taking this route. In the long run, however, your soul is being denied its nourishment, and your body, too, will never feel satisfied.

The second choice is to see your life as an intimate relationship with the Source of Life Above —as though every dollar earned was pure manna from heaven, handed to you personally and lovingly straight from the hand of your G-d and partner in all you do.

Then your main job will be to keep sparkling clean the basket where your manna will fall, insuring that no one is hurt or misled by your business. And to give of your profits to spread kindness in the world.

Maybe you'll get rich this way. Maybe you won't. But you will always be satisfied.

84) The Typist

To a mother who asked advice on becoming a typist to supplement the family income:

Don't *become* a typist. You are a mother.

Type, if you feel you need to in order to support your *family*. But don't *become* a typist.

85) In Sum

Be within.

But stay above.

STRUGGLE

Even if you fail to conquer the darkness entirely, even if you are still rolling in the mud with the enemy—you can still find G-d in the struggle itself.

After all, He is not only light. He is darkness as well.

86) Jealous Angels

The angels are jealous of the one who struggles in darkness.

They have light,
but he touches the Essence.

87) Cleaning Up

Everyone has his share of "not good." It's impossible that a physical being should be void of faults. The point is not to flee or hide from them. Nor is it to resign yourself to it all. It is to face up to the fact that they are there, and to systematically chase them away.

Recognizing who you are and gradually cleaning up your act—it may look ugly, but it is a divine path.

88) Congratulations

You cannot blame yourself, never mind persecute yourself for how you feel. But you can rejoice in the battle of controlling and sublimating those feelings.

Every small victory within you is a major triumph over the darkness of this world. Indeed, this is why this darkness was placed within you, in order that you may transform it into great light.

89) Consent

This is how that darkness within us finds its way out: First it agrees with everything good we do.

When we choose to meditate, it tells us,
"Yes! Meditate! That way you will become a great sage!"

When we choose to do a good deed, it says,
"Yes! You are so wonderful! Think what others will do in return for this!"

Slowly, slowly, it convinces us that any good we do requires its approval. And then, you've fallen into its trap.

Do good without reason. Then there are no traps.

90) Mockery

Mockery is the prime weapon of the dark impulses within Man. It is the prime obstacle to moving forward and upward —the thought that perhaps people will say, "Why are you behaving today differently than you did yesterday? Weren't you good enough then?
Are you really so great today?"

And the most powerful mocker
is the one within your own self.

When you start something you know is good and right, and you hear a voice inside saying,

"Hold it! Who do you think you are to take on such a lofty noble path? Hypocrite! Don't you remember what you were involved in just a moment ago?"

—know that what you did a moment ago is irrelevant.
All that matters is what you will do right now.

Any voice that holds you back from moving forward—no matter how justified it may sound
—any such voice is a voice of destruction and decay,
not of growth and life.

91) Hope

There is always hope.

Even when you mess up, you have not wrestled control from Him. After all the dust has settled, where you are and how you are is exactly as He had planned at the outset of creating this world.

And so, there is always hope.

92) With the Body

Fasting and punishing the body is not a path for our generation. Not only because most of us are too fragile to weaken our bodies any more. Not only because the faintness of hunger can interfere with your ability to do good in the world.

But principally because now has come the time to lead a spiritual life *with* the body rather than against it.

93) Not the Body

Remember you are not the body. Neither are you the animal that pounds within the body, demanding its way in every thing. You are a G-dly soul.

Do not confuse the pain and struggle of the body with the joy and purity of the G-dly soul.

94) Advice on Anger

Prepare yourself with this meditation, and when you feel anger overcoming you, run through it in your mind:

Know that all that befalls you comes from a single Source, that there is nothing outside of that Oneness to be blamed for any event in the universe.

And although this person who insulted you, or hurt you, or damaged your property—he is granted free choice and is held culpable for his decision to do wrong—

That is *his* problem. That it had to happen to *you*—that is between you and the One Above.

95) Animal Taming

You are the master over the animal within, not the slave.

Just because it burns inside like a furnace
doesn't mean you must obey.

96) The Rock

There are times when the entire world
denies the truth you know within.

There are times you must be a lion, a deer,
an eagle, a tree—but now you must be a rock.

Now you must not flinch, not in any way even acknowledge the existence of the mighty waves that come crashing down upon you, conspiring to grind you to sand, to sweep you away to join them in the vast ocean.

You must be the hard, unmoving rock that lies at the essence of your soul, the voice from beyond all this ephemeral reality, from beyond all time and space. The voice that says, "They are nothing.
There is none else but He."

It begins with you. And then it happens in your world: The outer crust of facade begins to crack, the essential reality is revealed, the storm dissipates as though it never were, and all things begin to say, "I am not a thing.
In truth, there is none else but He."

97) Intense Sparks

There are sparks of light hidden in this world. Some you can find and liberate: When you "Know G-d in all your ways"—finding Him in whatever you do—those sparks jump out at you and their light is released.

But then there are sparks of such intensity that they had to be buried in the deepest bowels of the material realm and locked away in thick darkness. These are sparks that no ordinary search could uncover: Your intellect has no power even to approach them. Your deeds could never dig that deep. Your eyes would be blinded by their brilliance and by the profundity of the darkness surrounding them.

The only tools you have to liberate those sparks are the ones that supersede your intellect and your senses. These are the inner powers that are revealed when your inner resolve brought to the test.

This is the reason our generation is so challenged again and again: We are redeeming the final sparks of light.

98) Choosing Life

Isn't this the whole meaning of life in this world:

To choose between bondage to the material world and believing that your life comes from those many forces—

—or to choose true life and to believe that all your needs and all your concerns come only from the one Source of All Life.

99) Between Hope & Trust

There is hope, and there is trust in G-d
—and they are two distinct attitudes.

Hope is when there is something to latch on to, some glimmer of a chance. The drowning man, they say, will clutch at any straw to save his life.

Trust in G-d is even when there is nothing in which to hope. The decree is sealed. The sword is drawn over the neck. By all laws of nature there is no way out.

But the One who runs the show
doesn't need any props.

100) Celebrate!

If you are confident that G-d will help you, then why is misery and anxiety written all across your face? If you are really confident, celebrate!

FROM DESPAIR TO JOY

Describing the joy of the Rebbe is something like describing the majesty of the Rocky Mountains to a prairie dweller. We think of happiness as all the outer trappings of smiley faces and the "having-a-good-time" look. But what we saw on the Rebbe was an inner joy—the sort of joy you feel when a sudden, brilliant light bulb flashes inside—except continual and constant. Not a joy that dissipates and burns itself out, but a tightly contained joy of endless optimism, power and life, waiting the special moment when it would burst forth like an unexpected tsunami, sweeping up every soul in its path.

Even now, if you would enter the Rebbe's private office, you would feel there the vitalizing joy that pervades the air and every object the Rebbe touched.

The Rebbe once confided that he himself was by nature a somber and introspective person. With hard work, he said, he was able to affect his spirit to be full of joy.

101) Denying Reality

Despair is the diametric opposite of everything in which we believe—in other words: it is a denial of reality.

It is a denial that there is a G-d that directs all of His creation and watches over every individual and assists each one in what he must accomplish.

102) Self-Destruction

Depression is not a crime. But it plummets a person into an abyss deeper than any crime could reach.

Depression is a ploy instigated by the self-destructive elements within all of us. Once depressed, a person could do anything.

Fight depression as a blood-sworn enemy. Run from it as you would run from death itself.

103) Higher & Closer

Despair is the ultimate form of self-worship—the perception that you have the capacity to truly mess up, to take the world's destiny out of its Creator's hands
and sabotage His plans.

Know that the world is in a constant state of elevation, rocketing upwards towards its ultimate wholeness at every moment. Every quivering of every leaf, every subtle breeze, every slightest motion of any particle of our universe is another move in that same direction.

Even those events that seem to thrust downward are in truth only a part of the ascent—like the poise of an athlete before he leaps, the contraction of a spring
before its energy is released.

There is not a thing you could do halt that dynamic even for a moment. True, you must take responsibility for your deeds and work hard, very hard, to clean up your own mess. But when all the dust settles, you are exactly in the space where you were meant to be:

One step closer.

104) Joy Unleashed

There are many kinds of barriers: Those from within and those from without. Barriers between people. Barriers that prevent you from doing good things. Barriers of your own mind and your own hesitations. There are the barriers that exist simply because you are a limited being.

Joy breaks through all barriers.

105) Simple Path

You ask, "How can I be happy if I am not?"

True, you can't control the way you feel,
but you do have control over your conscious
thought, speech and actions.

Do something simple: Think good thoughts, speak good things, behave the way a joyful person behaves—even if you don't fully feel it inside. Eventually, the inner joy of the soul will break through.

106) Joyful Prognostics

Having discovered all your faults, you are depressed.

Imagine you have just found a doctor with a diagnosis that explains all your afflictions over the past many years. And he's written a prescription directing you on a sure path to good health.

Shouldn't you jump with joy and relief?

107) Humble Joy

Much depression stems from haughtiness.

If you would realize who you really are,
you wouldn't be so disappointed with yourself.

108) Mind-full

You must always have good things to think about.

An empty mind is a vacuum awaiting destructive thoughts.

109) All of You

Where your thoughts are

there you are,

all of you.

110) Out of Center

If you think about yourself all day, you are guaranteed to become depressed.

Instead, take an hour a day to think of how you can benefit someone else.

111) Impact

Complacency breeds anxiety.

To be healthy, a person needs to be affecting his surroundings, uplifting those about him and bringing in more light.

112) Despair on Purpose

Despair is a cheap excuse

for avoiding one's purpose in life.

And a sense of purpose

is the best way to avoid despair.

113) Self-Confidence

To a young man who wrote he lacked self-confidence in dealing with others:

Sit with friends and work together with friends. Soon you will see you can do as well as them. Then the inner strength of your soul will begin to shine through.

114) Focus

Everything that occurs comes from Him, and He is only good. But if you and your world are not prepared to receive such good, it may manifest itself as apparent bad.

Struggle hard to see the good, think positively —and then the good will become revealed.

115) Childish Joy

The natural state of Man, the way G-d created him, is to be happy. Look at children and you will see.

116) Everything!

Everything must be done with joy.

Even remorse can be with joy.

117) In All Ways

People imagine a place of G-dliness as a place for seriousness, a solemn place, a place that fills you with trepidation.

The truth is, where there is G-d, there is joy.

That is why our every moment is a moment to celebrate and fill with joy. Because at every moment we are fulfilling our mission of bringing G-dliness into this world. Not just the obviously joyful matters, such as meditation, study, prayer and good deeds, but also regular, mundane activities and the ways we earn an income and go about life—all are ways by which we know Him and bring Him into our world.

118) Gratefulness

A person is happy when he knows something worthwhile belongs to him. A person is very happy when he feels he is small and yet he owns something very great.

We are all finite owners of the Infinite.

When I first showed this book to friends I detected a disdain for the phrase "serving G‑d"—a concept that comes up so often. After all, servitude went out of fashion with the Emancipation.

But I left the term in. This is not a book about friends' thoughts or even my own thoughts—this is about the Rebbe, and that's the term he used.

Servitude conjures a sense of surrendering one's being to another entity—thereby imprisoning all the potential of self-fulfillment you've been given. But when we talk about serving the very source of your being, the surrender of self takes on a whole new and opposite meaning.

In your source, you are infinite—as your Creator is infinite. Serving your Creator then reads as plugging in to the ultimate self, becoming one with the infinite, one with the Creator Himself.

119) The Infinite Connection

The purpose of every human being is to serve his Creator, and that is a service of great joy:

"I, puny mortal and decidedly finite being, serve with my deeds the Infinite Creator of All Worlds! I am bound to the Source of Life from birth, and all the many raging waters of this world cannot tear me away from that bond. Even if I sometimes fail, I may always return and in a single moment reconnect all my soul."

BRICK WALLS

It is a Jewish Custom on the holy day of Rosh Hashana to walk to a pond or river and recite certain prayers there.

In Brooklyn, finding such a body of water within walking distance can be a bit of a problem. In the early years of the Rebbe's leadership, there would be a whole parade every year to the Brooklyn Botanical Gardens.

One year, the rain poured incessantly and most assumed the walk cancelled. "Cancelled", however, was never part of the Rebbe's vocabulary. When the Rebbe came out for the walk, news traveled like lightning and people scrambled to join. Upon arrival at the gardens, however, they found the gates locked and nobody there to let them in.

The wall around the Brooklyn Botanical Gardens is fairly high. The Rebbe gazed up and said softly to his assistant, "How tall do you think that wall is?"

The assistant had no time to answer. The Rebbe was already climbing the wall.

As soon as they realized what was going on, those close by rushed to assist the Rebbe. He looked down and said, "If you will allow me to do this myself, I think I will be far more successful."

120) Going Over

Rabbi Shmuel of Lubavitch, known as "The Rebbe Maharash", the fourth in the golden chain of rebbes of Lubavitch, had an attitude.

Many wise people say if you can't go under, go over. The Rebbe Maharash said, "Just go over."

Meaning that instead of first trying to work through a problem by its own rules, and then—if that doesn't work—gathering the strength and courage to step brazenly over it…

…instead, just start by stepping right over it, as though there were no obstacle to begin with.

After all, that's why obstacles are there in the first place —so you will go higher.

121) Keep Going

On their exodus from Egypt, towards Mount Sinai, the Jewish People arrived at an obstacle—the Red Sea. They divided into four parties.

One prepared to fight.

One said to surrender and return.

One advocated mass suicide.

One began to pray.

G-d spoke to Moses and said, "Why are you crying out to me? I told you to travel straight ahead. Keep going and you will see there is no obstacle!"

The Jewish People kept going
and the obstacle became a miracle.

122) As Per Design

People think that G-d first made a world and then gave us instructions to follow, so we won't mess it up. The truth is, the instructions came first, and the world was designed as the venue to carry them out.

Therefore, to say that anything in the world could be an opposition to carrying out its Creator's will is an absurdity. There can be no opponents to the purpose of creation—only meaningful challenges.

123) Friendly Hardships

Hardships in life are the material world's way of beckoning to you, "Purify me! Elevate me!"

They come to you knowing you can overcome them, and thereby they will fulfill their purpose of being.

124) Serious Darkness

Don't take the world and its darkness so seriously—it is not as real as it feigns to be.

It is only a creation, regenerated out of absolutely nothingness at every moment.

The only thing *real* about it is its purpose of being —that you should purify it.

125) Chutzpah

This world operates on chutzpah.
It has the chutzpah to declare itself a world,
to assert that it is autonomous from its Creator,
to deny any relationship to the very force that is continually bringing it into being every moment.

- We will fight chutzpah with chutzpah.

126) Isometrics

The world is not obstructing you—it is challenging you.

It knows its deepest treasures can only be revealed by the deepest faculties of your soul, and it taps those powers by providing isometrics for the soul.

127) Another Chance

There's no such thing as defeat.
There's always another chance. To believe in defeat is to believe that there is something, a certain point in time that did not come from Above.

Know that G-d doesn't have failures. If things appear to worsen, it is only as part of them getting better.

We only fall down in order to bounce back even higher.

128) Adam's Challenge

Adam was the direct handiwork of G-d. No other human being could ever be as magnificent. Yet he had only one temptation to resist and he gave in.

Which teaches us that the greatest challenges in life are those that are closest to your purpose of being.

So that if you wish to know your primary purpose in life, you need only look at where you find your greatest challenge.

129) Fear

Captivity begins by believing that you are small
and the world is big.

Once you believe that, next you are likely to believe it will step on you, and you fear it.

And then you come to obey it, then to run after it. And then you are its slave, so that even as your soul thirsts for living waters, it cannot even begin to search for them.

To fear the world is to deny the Oneness of its Creator.

130) Inferiority

When the spies that Moses sent returned from their rendezvous of the Land of Canaan, they included in their report these words:

"We felt like ants before them,
and so we were in their eyes."

Because they felt like ants in their own eyes,
therefore, others saw them as ants as well.

131) Excuses

One who really cares is not placated by the fact that he has a good excuse.

If the goal was not achieved, it was not achieved—regardless of the excuse.

132) Not If, But How

Sometimes it may appear that there is a place where, according to all considerations, G-dliness can't come. An obstacle that prevents you from accomplishing something beneficial. A friend who cannot be approached to help do a favor. A gathering of people that seems meaningless.

The appropriate thing to do in such a situation is to throw out all considerations and just *do*.

Your job is not to determine *if* and *where*. Your job is to determine *how*.

Do, and you will see miracles.

133) Landing

To one who fell into enormous debt
trying to achieve miracles:

We were told to transcend limitations
—but that doesn't mean just jumping into the air with no
idea of where you're going to land!

COMING HOME

In the Rebbe's spiritual universe, there are no strangers to the Source of Life. It is not a place that is discovered, or that you come to as a tourist. There is only return. Reconnection.

The soul begins in an intimate, essential bond with a Source Beyond All Things. Even as she invests herself into a material world, into a human form, that primordial bond remains imprinted deep within her. It is that bond that pulls her constantly to return, like a magnet pulling its lost other half. All the searching of Man, all his spiritual striving, all is only an expression of this dynamic, this thirst to return.

The desire to return is innate, but it must be awakened. The soul must first realize she is distant. Return in all its strength and passion is found, therefore, in the soul who has wandered far from her true self and then awakened to recognize she is lost. We are like the child being pushed on a swing by her father—the further our souls are thrust away, the greater the force of our return.

As well, the drive to return is G‑d's fishing net. For in its search to reunite with Him, the soul finds G‑d in all the matters of this world. And so, these too are pulled in. And the deeper the descent, the greater the treasure.

134) The Rainbow

Our world is a world where a rainbow could be.

At first, there was a world that only received and returned no dividends. Its inhabitants took no ownership. They lived with their Creator's benevolence, they did what they did with no need for excuses, and eventually died as they died. And that was it.

With the Flood, this world was re-created. The earth was cleansed, the atmosphere purified. It became a world that could take the sunshine that poured in from above and refract it into many colors.

It became a world where a created being could be born, take the soul, body, share of the world and all the sustenance its Maker gave to it, *use* that, *do something* with that—and then return it, saying, "See what I have done with that which you gave me!"

And so, G-d vowed to never destroy the world again. For, if the inhabitants would go wrong, they might always turn around and clean up their own mess.

135) Failure

Adam trudged past the gates of Eden, his head low, his feet heavy with remorse and pain.

Then he stopped, spun around and exclaimed, "Wait a minute! You had this all planned! You put that fruit there knowing I would eat from it! This is all a plot!

There was no reply.

Without failure, Man can never truly reach into the depths of his soul. Only once he has failed, can he return and reach higher and higher without end. Beyond Eden.

136) Resilience

Success, in the higher scheme of things, is when a soul that has alienated herself returns. It is the ultimate demonstration of her resilience and her depth:

No matter how distant she may travel, in the end she can never tear herself away.

137) From the Core

Return is the ultimate act of self-expression.
Nobody returns because s/he is commanded to do so. The ability to return comes from you alone.

And that itself the evidence that you were never truly torn away: The outer garments of the soul may have been severed, but the core remained at every moment in intimate union with its Source.

And from there came the message to return.

138) Exploiting the Darkness

One who returns from the darkness must bring of that darkness and transform it to light.

One who returns from a place far from G-d must exploit his experience to surge higher and higher with greater strength.

Therefore, one who returns from a distant, dark place is greater than one who was always close.

It's not so much how high you've reached, but with what force you are moving in which direction.

139) Beyond the Darkness

In creating the whole of existence, G-d made forces that reveal Him and forces that oppose Him—He made light and He made darkness. One who does good brings in more light. One who fails, feeds the darkness.

But the one who fails and then returns transcends that entire scheme. He reaches out directly to the Essential Creator. Beyond darkness and light.

And so, his darkness becomes light.

140) Darkness Transformed

When light pushes away the darkness, eventually another darkness shall come.

When the darkness itself is transformed into light, it is a light that no darkness can oppose.

141) Return Beyond Time

To return takes but a moment.

One moment a being is at an ultimate distance from her G-d and from her true self, the next she is in complete union.

The power to return is beyond time.

142) Switch on the Light

A college student asked the Rebbe what is his job. The Rebbe gestured to the ceiling of his room and replied:

Do you see that light bulb? It is connected by wires to a power plant that powers the whole of Brooklyn. And that plant is connected to turbo-generators at Niagara Falls that power the whole of New York State and more.

Every one of us is a light bulb wired in to an infinitely powerful generator. But the room is still dark because the connection has not yet been made.

The job of a Rebbe is to take your hand in the dark room and help it find the switch.

143) Mentors

Every person needs a mentor. And that mentor needs a mentor. And that mentor as well—nobody pulls himself up by tugging at his own hair.

Go out and find yourself someone you can rely on for advice and counsel, someone who understands you and whom you can trust and respect. If that person turns you down, insist and persist. Don't wait to become a student. Be proactive and make someone into your teacher.

144) The Transparent Teacher

The true teacher connects you with your G-d —and then gets out of the way.

HEALING

Hundreds of letters arrived daily to the Rebbe asking for advice and blessing in medical matters. That there were miracles is undisputed. Gather together ten Jews anywhere in the world and one will have a story about a friend, a relative or perhaps his or her own self to whom a miracle of the Rebbe occurred.

But the Rebbe didn't want to make a religion out of miracle healing. With almost every response, he gave practical advice, generally encouraging people along a spiritual path together with a wise medical one. Here are a few of the more typical responses:

145) Soul Healing

People think that if they are not well, they must sacrifice all meaning in their life in order to take care of their physical situation. In fact, the opposite is true: You cannot separate the healing of the body from the healing of the soul. As you treat the body, you must also *increase* in nourishing the soul.

Doctors know this very well, but they should make better use of the fact.

146) Healthy Body, Healthy Soul

To serve G-d you need a healthy body as well as a healthy soul. How can you meditate, pray or study properly when the body's wellness is neglected?

Taking care of your body so that the soul can flourish is a divine service.

147) Blood Pressure

Don't be so upset with the world.

Anger at the world is anger at G-d,
and it's also bad for your blood pressure.

148) Doctor & Friend

Ask the advice of a doctor who is a friend.

Being a friend makes a big difference.

149) In Case of Doubt

In general, when doctors disagree, follow the opinion of the majority of the experts. But in the case of surgery, if there is uncertainty it is usually better to refrain and trust that the Healer of All Flesh will heal and strengthen you.

150) Miracles & Doctors

Firm confidence in G-d can perform miracles of healing. Nevertheless, you should still follow the instructions of the doctor.

Not that it is the doctor or his medicine that heals —it is the Healer of All Flesh who heals.

But the doctor and the medicine provide a natural channel for the healing to occur, and this is the way G-d prefers His miracles to work—through natural means.

151) Four Steps

Four things advised for healing:

Find a good doctor and follow his instructions.

- Dispel any thoughts about illness.
- Think only healthy thoughts.

Strengthen your confidence in the Healer of All Flesh, that He will heal you in whatever way He sees fit.

Increase your study of the inner light of Torah.

152) Medical License

To one who was given an ominous prognosis:

- The doctor has been licensed from Above to heal, not to make predictions.

- Ignore the predictions and think only good thoughts.

BREAKING FREE

In Russia, for 70 years, the life of an observant Jew was a perpetual act of martyrdom. Leading your life the way you knew it was supposed to be led meant carrying the weight of the Kremlin and the KGB ominously over your head, with the constant threat of arrest, torture and exile to Siberia. It meant every week risking another strategy to avoid work on Saturday, teaching your children in a different secret cellar each day, suffering scorn and ridicule for being who you were.

Then they came to America. And they could not find the enemy.

It is not a problem unique to chassidim, but to people in general who migrated to a new world and just couldn't see the connection between all this and what they had left behind. How do you pass on to the next generation something that doesn't seem to fit in this new context even for yourself?

This is a task where the human mind finds great difficulty: Relating familiar ideas to a new, completely unfamiliar time and place. We are dragged helplessly by the current of Time, mercilessly ripped from our hold on the past that fathered us, forcibly confronting a future with no chance to prepare. We are the intimidated victims, servants and prisoners of Time, forever bowing to the pressures of the moment.

But then there are souls that remain beyond the realm of time and place, even while they enter into it. They know Time as one who looks down from the highest mountain, watching as snow becomes creek becomes river becomes sea. To them there is no dissonance, no conflict—only the movements of a magnificent symphony.

Into our time entered the Rebbe.

Those who could see no further than their own optic nerve saw the Rebbe as a relic of the past. With an untainted eye it was obvious that to the Rebbe there is no past.

To others, life in the small Jewish settlements of Europe had no relevance to the new life in America. The Rebbe saw the essence of that life, and the essence doesn't change.

To others, the time and place of martyrdom had ended, and an era of freedom and self-indulgence had begun. To the Rebbe, it is all just a newer and even higher rung on the ladder of transcendence of the self.

153) The New Self-Sacrifice

The last written work of the Rebbe before his stroke centered on the following thought. The Rebbe personally handed a copy to thousands of people. I believe it is a summary of who we are and what we must do:

Self-sacrifice in a land of freedom penetrates to the bone.

I saw men and women who sacrificed all they had
to defy the religious persecution of the Bolshevik regime.
They came to a land of freedom and comfort
—where is their greatness now?

Then there is the child of that land of freedom and comfort, worshipping it, chasing after it—but inside he is crushed by the spiritual void. His inner being does not let him alone, the spark inside that cries, "This is not what I really want! I don't want this world! I don't want any worlds! All I want is Him alone!"

This is the crushing of an olive for its oil. The oil spreads and penetrates every fiber of his being. His every faculty begins to burn. And there shines the source of light that can never be extinguished nor dimmed.

It is the light from which a new age is formed.

154) Self-Surrender

They think self surrender means to say, "I have no mind. I have no heart. I only believe and follow, for I am nothing."

This is not self-surrender—this is denial of the truth. For it is saying there is a place where G-dliness cannot be—namely your mind and your heart.

G-d did not give you a brain that you should abandon it, or a personality that you should ignore it. These are the building materials from which you may forge a sanctuary for Him, to bring Divine Presence into the physical realm.

Don't run from the self with which G-d has entrusted you. Connect your entire being to its Essential Source. Permeate every cell with the light of self-surrender.

155) Small Things

Great things are not what is demanded from our generation. The previous generations did all that for us. We need only do the small things—but in a more difficult time.

For us, self-sacrifice could mean nothing more than a simple change of habit.

156) Subliminal Surrender

Self-surrender doesn't mean jumping off a bridge.
Self surrender means surrendering the self.
Putting aside the "I want", the "I need",
the "I think such-and-such."
Even the "I am."

Self-surrender is the subliminal drive behind all sincerely good deeds. Today, as materialism reigns and the human spirit is darkened, that powerful drive can no longer stay undercover.

157) Confidence & Humility

Confidence is best found among the truly humble.

Moses was the most humble of all men. Yet he had the confidence to stand before the mightiest dictator on earth and assert his demands. He had the confidence to stand before G-d and listen without losing his composure. He had the confidence even to argue with G-d, when necessary.

Yet he considered himself to be nothing.

The confidence of Moses was not confidence in his own self. He had no self. He was but an agent of Above.
Above there is infinite power.

Self-confidence is limited, at best. But if you trust in the One who has sent you to be here and do what you need to do—that confidence knows no bounds.

158) Authentic Humility

Humility has to be real.

Real humility means transcendence of the self.

Moses, it is written, was the most humble of all men.

Obviously, he knew who he was. He knew that of all men, he alone was chosen to accomplish the greatest tasks of history—to lead an entire nation out from bondage and bring them to the greatest revelation that would ever be. He was the loftiest of all prophets, who spoke directly to G-d whenever he wished.

He knew all this and yet he was humble.

Because Moses told himself, "This is not my own achievement. This is what I have done with the powers G-d has granted me. Had someone else been given these same powers, perhaps that someone else would have done a better job."

159) The Sewing Needle

Man is G-d's needle to sew the many patches of Creation into a single garment for His glory.

At one end, the needle must be hard and sharp, to squeeze through the ordeal. But the other end must have a vacant hollow, a nothingness with which to hold the thread.

With the world, be firm and sharp.
Within, feel how small you are before the Infinite.

160) Joy

One who feels himself cannot feel joy.

161) The Highest

True happiness is the highest form of self-sacrifice. There, in that state, there is no sense of self—not even awareness that you are happy. True happiness is somewhere beyond "knowing." Beyond self.

All the more so when you bring joy to others.

162) The Gateway

A sense of nothingness doesn't mean being everybody's doormat. In fact, just the opposite: A sense of nothingness is your gateway to infinite powers.

163) Prisoners

We are all prisoners. But we sit on the keys.

Finitude is our cell.

The universe is our prison.

Our jail keeper is the Act of Being.

The keys to liberation are clenched tightly

in the fists of our own egos.

164) Beyond I

The primordial blunder was the discovery of self.

The first man and woman in the Garden of Eden ate of the Tree of Knowledge and realized that they exist.
Ever since then, that self-consciousness has been the root of every disaster.

Every "I" and "me", every sense of being is a denial of the Oneness of the Creator and the creation. It is a statement that there is something else, namely *me*, and I am autonomous from all this.

The goal of mankind is to reach beyond the state of Adam and Eve in the Garden—to a state where any sense of ego is meaningless. A place called Eden, beyond the Garden, the place of Essential Being from where all delights flow…

"And a river went out from Eden to water the Garden."

And now you know why they ate of the fruit to begin with.

165) Leaving Egypt

The biblical slavery of Egypt represents bondage to your own self.

Every day, every moment, must be an exodus from the self.

If you're not leaving Egypt, you're already back there.

166) Four Realms

The ancient philosophers divided the world into four realms, each realm transcendental in a way beyond those that precede it:

The "silent" realm—earth, rocks, water, air, etc., do not transcend their bounds in any way.

Plants transcend their bounds by growing.

Animals transcend their bounds by traversing space.

And Man, how does he transcend his bounds?
Man reaches outside of himself with words.
With dialogue.

Man alone is capable of hearing his own self through the ears of another. Man alone is capable of transcending the very bounds of self.

167) Escape

Make a part of your life an act that takes you beyond your bounds—helping people that are *not* part of your family or circle of friends, doing something that does *not* fit within your own self-definition.

Escape yourself.

168) Fur Coats and Fireplaces

Have you ever heard of the "Saint in a Fur Coat"?

He sits in his house by a fireplace full of wood. But there is no fire. The house, and everyone in it are shivering from the cold. All except for him. He dons a fur coat and he is warm.

So we ask him, "Why do you warm only yourself?
Why not kindle the wood in your fireplace and warm others as well?"

He answers, "It is not just this house. The entire world is struck with a bitter, cold wind. Do you expect me to warm up an entire world?"

So we tell him that he does not have to warm up the entire world. But perhaps he could warm up one other individual. Perhaps two. Perhaps he could warm up one little *corner* of the world.

"For a person such as I," he replies, "it is not fitting to warm up only one corner."

And so there he sits, in his cold, dark house,
all comfy in his fur coat.

169) Noah & Abraham

When G-d told Noah to build an ark before the world would be destroyed, Noah built an ark.

But when G-d told Abraham He was about to destroy the cities of Sodom and Gomorra—cities corrupt and evil to the core. Abraham argued. He said, "Perhaps there are righteous people there! Will the Judge of All the Earth not do justice?"

Abraham felt a sense of ownership for the world in which he lived. If there was something wrong, it needed to be changed. Even if it had been decreed by the will of G-d.

170) & Moses

Moses took ownership of the dark as well as the light. He argued not just for the righteous, but also for those who had failed.

When the people angered G-d with a golden calf only 40 days after the revelation of Absolute Oneness at Mount Sinai, Moses had to admit they had wronged. Yet he did more than plead for them: He put his entire being on the line for them.

"Forgive them!" he demanded.

"And if you do not forgive them, then wipe me out from Your book that You have written!"

171) The Ultimate Sacrifice

The Rebbe wept profoundly as he spoke these words:

The entire being of Moses was the Torah he brought to his people. The Torah was more than something he taught. It was what he was. It was his G-d within him.

Yet when it came to a choice between the Torah and his people, he chose his people. He said, "And if you do not forgive them, then wipe me out from Your book that You have written!"

His whole being was the Torah,
but deep into his essence, at the very core,
was his oneness with his people.

172) Ego Dieting

Doing good is not about being nice.

You can do nice things all day long for many people, but it could be all just more service of your own self, food for your own ego.

The world was designed so people would need each other, not so you could be nice, but to give you the opportunity to escape the confines of your own self.

When you help those who show gratitude, when you lend a hand to those who are on your side, you are still within the realm of your own ego and self.

- Help someone you don't want to help. Help him and learn to want to help him—only because this is the right thing to do.

At first, it may not feel so rewarding.
But you have sprung free.

173) Beyond the Possible

We all have limitations—after all, we live in physical bodies.

- There comes a time, however, when you have to break out beyond those limits; you've got to do more than you can possibly do.

- The truth is, you are more than a body. You are a G-dly soul—and G-dliness knows no limits.

174) Free Love

There are people who believe they are doing good by swallowing other's egos alive. The egos of those they cannot help, and of those who cannot help them, are inedible to them—and therefore intolerable. They cannot work *with* others—because their egos leave no space for "others"—only for those extensions of their own inflated selves that show they *need* them, or for those whom *they* need.

You don't love your neighbor to glorify your own ego. When you come to your sister or brother's aid, leave your own self behind. Love with self-sacrifice.

175) Sincerity

When you and the path you have chosen get along just great, it's hard to know whether your motives are sincere.

But when you come across a path to do good, and you see this path goes against every sinew of your flesh and every cell in your brain, when you want only to flee and hide from it—*do this*.

Then you shall know your motives are sincere.

176) Liberated by Betrothal

In truth, the world, standing on its own,
is a place of exile and captivity.

Even when a man stands upright on the tallest mountain and perceives all there is to perceive, comprehends all that can be comprehended, achieves a realization of the Ultimate Oneness and Void that is behind all this—

But in the end, he is still stuck on the ground where his feet have brought him, his eyes have not seen beyond his own eyeballs, his mind has only comprehended that which he can know and reached that which is reachable—he has remained within his own self.

And the proof :
he has remained with a G-d Who is above
and an earth which is below, and the two cannot meet.

- His only liberation, and the only liberation of the entire world, is when the One Above reaches down and tells us, "Do this. With this deed you are betrothed to Me."

And then there is no above and below.
Then there is only One.

177) The Rope

Man, on his own, cannot reach higher than his own ego. He cannot break out of his own skin; he cannot lift himself up by pulling at his own hair. All of his achievements are tied to his own ego. All that he may comprehend is defined by his own subjective perception. He is a prisoner by virtue of existence.

So G-d threw Man a rope:
He gave him tasks to fulfill that are beyond his comprehension; thoughts to fathom that take him outside the hollow of his subjective universe.

All that is needed is his willingness to leave himself.

We are all prisoners. But we sit on the keys.

178) Your Will

If you do His will only because it makes sense to you, then what has it got to do with Him? You are doing *your* will. You're back in prison.

179) A Fire

A person must be on fire—the fire of an altar burning up the ego inside, bringing the animal close to the divine.

A large ego burning makes a lot of noise.

A small ego burns quietly.

180) Smaller

"Rebbe! Nobody gives me respect! Everybody steps all over me and my opinions!"

— "And who told you to fill the entire space with yourself, so that wherever anyone steps, they must step on you?"

181) Nothingness

Nothingness is the medium through which all energy moves, from above to below and from below to above.

Below, in Man, a sense of nothingness that transcends ego. Above, a Nothingness that transcends all boundaries and planes.

The nothingness below fuses with the Nothingness above, locking heaven and earth in eternal embrace.

That is why G-d is found amongst the truly humble.

182) Small & Infinite

Make yourself small and you will be greater.

Know you are nothing and you will be infinite.

At the very least, don't make such a big deal of yourself and you will be all that much closer to the truth.

183) G-d in Exile

We are imprisoned because we have exiled our G-d.

As long as we search for G-d by abandoning the world He has made, we can never truly find Him.

As long as we believe there is a place to be escaped, there is no true liberation.

The ultimate liberation will be when we open our eyes to see that everything is here now.

184) Under Guard

It is there inside.

Everything is there inside.

But the "I" stands firmly guard at the gate.

TRUTH

In the beginning, people looked at the world about them in wonder. Then they began to make sense of whatever they could. But the wonder persisted. Eventually, they came to believe they could understand everything, that whatever does not make sense is simply not true—it does not exist. That's when the wonder died.

Truth is something you find when you surrender yourself to it. Truth is often something you would rather reject, something that refuses to sit inside your mind. Truth comes from somewhere beyond your grasp, beyond "you."

Once you have recognized that yes, this is the inescapable truth, then you must engage every cell of your brain to understand, to digest it. But begin with wonder, with emptiness, with eyes and ears open to that which the world is telling you.

185) Fools

To fool the world is one thing,
but to fool yourself is no big deal.

You're a fool for wanting to fool yourself
—and anyone can fool a fool.

186) Small Truths

People think that to attain truth you have to pulverize boulders, move mountains and turn the world upside-down. It's not so. Truth is found in the little things.

On the other hand, to move a mountain takes some dynamite and a few bulldozers. To do one of those little things can take a lifetime of working on yourself.

You do what you can: Learn and meditate and pray and improve yourself in the ways you know how—and He will help that what you do will be with Truth.

187) Higher Truth

There are many truths. There is a truth for every being and for every particle of the universe—for each one reflects its Master in a different way.

To seek truth means more than finding your own truth. It means finding a truth that works for you and for the other guy, for now and forever, in this place and everywhere, for the body and for the soul, for the sage and for the young, innocent child.

The higher the truth, the fewer boundaries it knows.

188) Two Paths

The Baal Shem Tov taught there are two paths:

G-dliness is everything.

Everything is G-dliness.

Where the two paths converge, there is G-d Himself.

189) Jacob's Path

G-dliness is everything is the path of Abraham. Abraham understood that there is a Reality beyond all realities, before which no existence is true. Therefore, he smashed the idols and declared to all people and in all places that there is only One.

Everything is G-dliness is the path of Isaac.
Isaac saw that the world is in truth G-dly. Therefore, Isaac dug wells, in the earth and in the people. He dug away the darkness and found the spark of G-dliness within each thing.

Jacob struggled with the darkness.

190) The Third Path

Each path contains what the other is missing: When G-dliness is everything, even the darkness is included. But the world is left unchanged, because there is no world—only G-dliness.

When everything is G-dliness, you transform the world by digging away the darkness to find the sparks of G-dliness. But the darkness remains piled up outside.

The path of Jacob is to find *That Which Is Everything* within each thing, and to bring *That Which Is Beyond All Things* to dwell within each thing. Jacob knows a G-d who is at once both beyond and within.

To Jacob, darkness is also light.

191) The Harder Easier Path

There are two paths you could take:
An easier path or a harder one.

Knowing that G-d is everything, you may wish to reject all the world stands for. Since everything is emptiness, you may deny yourself even necessities, living far and removed from the banalities of mankind, engaging only in the truths of the spirit, running from the confines of physical, mundane life.

This is the easier path.

On the other hand, knowing that within each thing G-d can be found, you may be inspired to refine and elevate our world, struggling with all its facets to find their true purpose, grabbing every opportunity to squeeze out a little more of the world's inherent good, living a spiritual life by using physical things in an enlightened way.

Both paths are true paths, and great sages have tread them both. But the second, more difficult one is the one we will all have the most benefit from, especially today.

192) Interface

All that exists
is Him
and you.

Everything else is just interface.

193) Three Possibilities

Everything that exists in your world is about communion with the Infinite. Each thing must be one of three:

A means to connect.

A path to fall away.

Or neutral ground
—awaiting you to transform it into a connection.

But if something were not part of your purpose,
it would not exist in your world.

194) The Other's World

In your world, all that exists is the Infinite and you.
In the world of your neighbor, all that exists is the Infinite and him. And his world is just as true as yours.

In the world of a cow, there's just the Infinite and it.
So with an insect, so with a plant, so even with a rock.

Every seat of consciousness constitutes a world.
And each world is true.

Knowing this is also part of your world:
The knowledge that in the other person's world you are only an accessory, an interface by which he connects.
And now you know how to enter his world.

195) Inner Peace

The world is a place of constant change and unrest.

Each point in time is distinct from the point before and the point after. Every point in space is its own world, with its own conditions and state of being. It is a world of fragments constantly rushing like traffic in anarchy.

Look at your own life: You do so many different things, one after the other without any apparent connection between them.

Inner peace is when every part of you and every facet of your day is moving in the same direction.

When you have purpose, you have peace.

196) The Child

This after 90 years soaked in Kabbalah and philosophy:

The ultimate prayer is the prayer of the small child.

You pray to some lofty concept of The Infinite Light or The Essence of Being or…

But the child doesn't have any concept. Just G-d.

…

- When you open your eyes in the morning,
  you are a newborn child.
  Then and there you meet G-d face to face.

  As you awaken and your brain becomes engaged, keep the child with you.

197) The Source

The Light was concealed.

But its Source was not.

The Source of Light is everywhere.

198) Who Owns Truth

•A sharp mind will find a truth for itself.

A humble spirit will find a truth higher than itself.

Truth is not the property of intellectuals, but of those who know how to escape their own selves.

199) Earthly Truth

Where is Truth?

When Man was made, it protested
and was thrown to the ground.
From there it sprouts forth.

Therefore, although many things appear true in spirit,
the ultimate test of truth is here on earth.

200) All or No One

No man can claim to have reached the ultimate truth
as long as there is another who has not.

No one is redeemed
until we are all redeemed.

Ultimate truth is an unlimited light
—and if it is unlimited,
how could it shine in one person's realm
and not in another's?

201) Simple & Earnest

The essential teaching of the Baal Shem Tov:

- Be simple, be earnest, and spread that simplicity throughout everything you do.

Simplicity is a receptacle for G-d's simple Oneness.

HIGHER LIFE

Originally, this chapter was titled, "Afterlife." Then I came across the Rebbe's response to a college student who asked for an explanation of afterlife.

The Rebbe replied that there is no such thing. Life doesn't end, it just continues in a higher form.

202) Heaven

We don't say a person "will be going to heaven." We say this person is "a child of the world to come."

Heaven is not just somewhere you go. It is something you carry with you.

203) Hell

*Everything about the Rebbe was pure kindness.
Even his idea of hell was as kind and generous as could be:*

People have a misconception of Hell. Let me tell you what Hell really is.

Hell is a spiritual place where everything that exists in our world exists, but in an infinite way.

So, whatever you chased after in this world, there you do it ad infinitum.

And that's Hell.

204) The Journey Home

Afterlife is a very rational, natural consequence of the order of things. After all, nothing is ever lost—even the body only transforms into earth. But nothing is lost.

The person you are is also never lost. It only returns to its source.

If your soul became attached to the material world during its stay here, then it must painfully rip itself away to make the journey back. But if it was only a traveler, connected to its source all along, then its ride home is heavenly.

205) High Souls

To one whose self is his body, death of the body is death of the self. But for one whose self is his love, awe and faith, there is no death, only a passing. From a state of confinement to the body he makes the passage to liberation. He continues to work within this world, and even more so than before.

The Talmud says that Jacob, our father, never died. Moses, also, never died. Neither did Rabbi Judah, the Prince. They were very high souls who were one with Truth in an ultimate bond—and since Truth can never die, neither could they.

Yes, in our eyes we see death. A body is buried in the ground and we must mourn the loss. But this is only part of the falseness of our world. In the World of Truth they are still here as before.

And the proof: We are still here. For if these high souls would not be with us in our world, all that we know would cease to exist.

206) Connecting

A true master of life never leaves this world—he transcends it, but he is still within it. He is still there to assist those who are bonded with him with blessing and advice, just as before, and even more so. Even those who did not know him in his corporeal lifetime can still create with him an essential bond.

The only difference is in us:
Now we must work harder to connect.

207) Self-Trial

The Baal Shem Tov taught that in the heavenly court there is no one who can judge you for what you have done in your life on earth. So this is what they do:

They show you someone's life—all the achievements and all the failures, all the right decisions and all the wrongdoings—and then they ask you, "So what should we do with this somebody?"

And you give your verdict. Which they accept. And then they tell you that this somebody was you. Being now in heaven, you don't recall a thing.

Of course, those who tend to judge others favorably have a decided advantage.

Better get in the habit now.

WE ARE ALL ONE

In his latter years, the Rebbe would stand for hours every Sunday, as thousands of people, both Jew and non-Jew would stand in line to receive his blessing. The Rebbe would look each person intently straight in the eyes for an eternal moment, often smiling, sometimes answering a question or providing advice, always giving his blessing or answering "amen" to the person's own request. Each person received from the Rebbe's hand a dollar bill to be given to any worthy cause of his or her choice.

All agreed that the spectacle was entirely supernatural. As the line went on, the Rebbe became increasingly invigorated, as though he himself was receiving life from these people. When, after many hours, the line would finally dwindle away, the Rebbe would turn to his personal secretary and ask, "Is there no one else?"

It happened one day that an elderly woman waited in line, sitting upon a small chair, which she moved ahead together with the line. When she finally arrived before the Rebbe, she could no longer contain herself. "Rebbe, I am younger than you!" she burst out. "And I only sat…and you stand here and greet each person… and just look at you!"

The Rebbe beamed and replied, "When you're counting jewels you don't get tired."

208) Handshake

I offer my hand of five fingers and you offer yours. Together we have a complete ten.

This is a handshake:
You and I are only fragments of the whole
—until we come together.

209) Fragments

We are all fragments of greater souls, and those souls fragments of even more lofty ones, and so on with those — until we all link back to the one primordial soul: The soul of Adam.

None of us is complete. No one can stand on his or her own. What one is lacking the other fulfills, where one excels, another is wanting.

Only together can we find oneness in our own selves. Only together can we be a fit vessel for the One Above to be revealed.

210) True Love

- The souls are all one. Only the bodies divide us.

  Therefore, one who places the body before the spirit can never experience true love or friendship.

211) Two Ones

- In two ways, we are one:
  In our essence, and in our character.

  In our essence, we are all one soul, with one source.

  In our character, we are all complimentary of each other, none of us complete, each one contributing what the other lacks, each one adding his touch of perfection to his fellow. Like a massive jigsaw puzzle, we fit together to make a single perfect whole.

  None of us is perfect without all the rest of us.
  And all the rest of us are incomplete when a single individual is missing.

212) In Trouble Together

Once, I came home to find my children climbing into the attic through a hole in the ceiling—an act I had sternly forbidden due to the dangers involved. But I watched before I opened my mouth. It took four of them: Two to lift one up and another to hold the chair those two were standing on. It was then that I understood something I had heard my Rebbe say many times:

When a father sees his children working together with love, he is prepared to forgive them for anything.

Better harmonious troublemaking than acrimonious obedience.

213) Which is Greater

They asked the Alter Rebbe:
"Which is greater: Love of G-d,
or love of your fellow man?"

"Love of your fellow man.
For then you are loving that which your Beloved loves."

214) Trust for Others

- Keep your trust in G-d to yourself. When things don't go so well, tell yourself it is all really for the good, and rejoice in however G-d treats you.

- But when others come with their troubles, telling them they should rejoice in their afflictions is plain callousness. Cry with them, pray for them, do everything you can for them—and *then* you can tell them to trust in G-d.

215) Hypocrisy

Do not be dismayed by the hypocrisy of others, nor by your own inconsistencies. Our lives are all journeys through hills and valleys—no man's spiritual standing is a static affair.

But the good each person achieves is eternal, as he connects to the Source of All Good, Who is infinite and everlasting. The failures, on the other hand, are transient and superficial, fleeting shadows of clouds, as stains in a garment to be washed away.

216) Not Doing

There are times when love can kill. There are times when you love someone so much, you cannot allow him to breath. He must do things the way *you* understand is best for him—because you cannot bear that one you love so much should be in any way distant from the truth as you know it.

"After all," you imagine, "I must do for him what I would have done for myself!"

But true love makes room for the one you love.

True love is best expressed not in what you do and what you say, but in what you *do not* do, and what you *do not* say.

217) Wanton Love

One who is full of himself fills all the space around him. There is no room left for anyone else. Therefore, he despises another person by virtue of the space that other person consumes. He may give reasons for his disdain, but the reasons are secondary.

This is called *wanton hatred*. It is the reason given for our exile. It is the core of all evil. It is balanced and cured by wanton acts of love and kindness.

218) Spontaneous

Someone wrote that he had, in his administrative duties, taken an action that fiercely angered one of his associates and turned him against him. The Rebbe replied:

Bring into your heart a deep love of this man, and his anger will spontaneously disappear.

219) Phase Two

The first stages of your life are to learn to be a master over yourself. But then comes a major and difficult transition in life, when you take on the responsibilities of a family. Now you must learn to put aside your own self-improvement for their sake.

220) Ego Activist

To someone who wrote he was avoiding social activism because it had been feeding his ego:

"And without the activism there is no ego? Better a haughty activist than a self-centered do-nothing!"

221) Tolerance

People misunderstand the meaning of tolerance.

Tolerance doesn't mean seeing someone harming himself and saying, "Live and let live." That's indifference. Apathy. If you see someone going the wrong way and you care about him, you'll do everything you can to set him straight.

Tolerance means that although you see his faults in all their ugliness naked before you, that doesn't decrease by one iota your respect for him as a fellow human being, and for all the good he has within him.

And if you say, "How can I be expected to lead a life of paradox, to both respect and rebuke at once?"

Let me ask you, do *you* have any faults? And do you not respect yourself nonetheless?

If you can live a life of paradox for yourself, you can give at least that privilege to the other guy.

222) Helping

Until you can see the good within a person,
you are incapable of helping him.

223) Words From the Heart

If you rebuke your brother and he does not listen,
then it is you who is to blame.

Words from the heart enter the heart.

224) Power Talk

Talk is powerful. Speak badly about someone and you expose all the ugliness in him, in yourself and in whoever happens to be paying attention. Once exposed, the wound begins to fester and all are hurt.

Speak good about the same person, and the inner good within him, within you and within all who participate begins to shine.

225) Delight to Anguish

Looking from the heavenly realm, all G-d's creatures look very good. He has great delight in all He has made.

But when one person makes a point of another's faults, that heavenly delight is transformed into a cloud of pain and anguish—over the very head of the one who spoke those words.

226) Helpful Knowledge

The very fact you know about someone who is in trouble means that in some way you are able to help. Otherwise, why would this knowledge have entered your world?

227) Dig Deeper

Every person you meet has a wellspring deep inside.

If you can't find it, the fault is yours.
Remove the rust from your shovel, sharpen its blade, and dig harder and deeper.

228) Uncovered and Shining

Our souls cannot be broken that they should need repair, nor deficient that they should need anything added.

Our souls need only to be uncovered and allowed to shine.

229) Mirrors

People are mirrors for each other.
 If you see the faults of another person and they don't leave you alone, it is truly your own faults you see.

This is G-d's great kindness to us, for without this device we would never be able to determine our true faults.

230) Special Soldiers

One of the most unforgettable talks I ever heard from the Rebbe was the time he spoke to the handicapped Israeli soldiers. Make that, "the special Israeli soldiers."

Each and every person is given all he needs to accomplish his mission in this world. But each of us have different missions, and therefore need different powers to accomplish them. Yet none of us has an easier time than any other.

Therefore, if you see a human being who appears deficient or "handicapped", know that in truth this person must have compensatory powers others do not have.
Do not call him "handicapped"—call him "special."

231) Thank You

An Israeli soldier lost his two legs when a Syrian land mine exploded beneath his jeep.

His mother came to him in the hospital and cried.

His father sat silent.

Generals and leaders came and made their speeches to him proclaiming him a hero and one to be proud of.

There was no condolence. The people still avoided him in the street.

The Rebbe shook his hand, looked him straight in the eye and said, "Thank you."

The "thank you" is still carrying him.

ACTS OF BEAUTY

When I was a kid, radical political activism was cool. By age fourteen, I was heavily involved.

But no matter how much you did, there was always this classic dilemma of "Hey, I'm only one out of six billion! And so is the guy next to me. It just does not seem plausible we could really make a difference!"

It didn't matter that you saw with your own eyes how much could be accomplished, that you had case histories to demonstrate how one person could turn around an entire world. It's a matter of cognitive dissonance—something the human mind simply cannot accept until some explanation is given.

The Rebbe gave an explanation: My problem was that I was only looking at the physical, observable world, but not what's behind it —somewhat analogous to seeing the control panel and not the engine. Sure, the deed is something that happens in the concrete, mundane world, but where there is a heart and soul behind the deed, then there is an effect deep within the metaphysical bowels of the natural order. So, just as one small button can trigger global reaction, one small deed can generate earth-shaking results.

232) Powerful Beauty

Never underestimate the power
of a simple, pure deed done from the heart.

The world is not changed by men who move mountains, nor
by those who lead revolutions,
nor by those whose purse strings tie up the world.

Dictators are deposed,
oppression is dissolved,
entire nations are transformed
by a few precious acts of beauty
performed by a handful of unknown soldiers.

In fact, it was Maimonides who wrote in his code of law, "Each person must see himself as though the entire world were held in balance and any deed he might do could tip the scales."

233) Light Power

All that came into being...

...all the created worlds and all the ethereal entities that live in them, even the worlds that are mere emanations without tangible substance, even the worlds of thought and beyond to the realms of infinite light that preceded Creation...

—all this came to be only as a result of the thought of you, the earthly being, struggling in a world that only a infinitesimal glimmer of G-dliness has reached in its purity, bringing light where light could not be.

And so it follows, that with one simple act of beauty, all those worlds and angels and realms of light become liberated and elevated and reciprocate with a burst of illumination into our lowly world.

That is why the entire creation can be transformed with one simple, sincere deed.
Never underestimate the power of light.

234) Mountain Climbing

At the final ascent,

he clings to any crack or crevice

to pull higher.

That is where we are now:

Any spark of light that comes your way,

squeeze all you can from it.

235) Without Measure

As soon as you start measuring good deeds, to determine which is greater, which takes priority over the other —you have already entered precarious ground.

Your job is to do whatever is sent your way.

236) Interest From G-d

Some people think that if they did something beautiful yesterday, or last week, or even several years ago, they've done their part and G-d should continue paying them for it the rest of their life. It's something like loaning money—you lend it to someone last year and you're still making a profit off him today.

Problem is, the Torah prohibits charging interest —even from G-d.

If you did good yesterday, do twice as good today.

237) Uncharity

Do not give charity.

Giving charity means being nice and giving away your money. But who says it is your money to begin with?
It is money put in your trust, to be disbursed for good things and for others when they will need it.

Change your attitude. Instead of doing what is nice, do what is *right*. Put the money where it belongs.

238) Unpraying

Do not pray.

Prayer means there are two entities,
one entity petitioning a higher one.

Instead of praying, connect. Become one with your Maker, so that divine energy will come through you and into our world to heal the sick, to cause the rain to fall…

239) Unrepenting

Do not repent.

Repentance means to stop being bad
and to become good.

But your essential being is always good.
The bad is only on the outside.
So instead of repenting, return.
Return to the essential self and to what is rightfully yours.

240) Givers & Takers

Our view of the world and its Creator's view
are very different.

From our perspective, there is always a giver and a taker. Whether the merchandise be knowledge, affection, or money—somebody always comes out on top and the other on the bottom.

In the Creator's view, giver and taker are one. The taker is really giving and the giver receiving. For without the opportunity to give, the giver would be forever imprisoned within his own self.

241) Humble Compassion

There is compassion that feeds the ego and there is compassion that humbles it.

Compassion that feeds the ego is a sense of pity for those who stand beneath you.

Compassion that humbles is born of a deeper understanding of the order of things:

When you understand that your fellow man is suffering in order that you may be privileged to help him
—then you are truly humbled.

242) Detoured Good

Sometimes it happens that you set out to do something with the best of intentions—and you end up with what appears the opposite.

Know with absolute certainty—because this is a tradition of our sages—that if your true intent is good, then only good can come out of it. Perhaps not the good you intended—or care for—but good nevertheless.

243) Higher & Higher

The Rebbe's most common response to someone who had done something positive:

It is our nature, all of us, that we never attain half our goal. If we earn $100, we must make $200. And when we reach $200, we strive for $400.

If so, our acts of kindness must grow by the same rules.

244) Beyond Reason

The world is not a reasonable place.
Meet it on its own terms: When you do something good, do it beyond reason.

245) Infinite Opportunity

Every moment,

every human activity

is an opportunity to connect with the Infinite.

Every act can be an uplifting of the soul.

It is only your will that may stand in the way.

But as soon as you wish,

you are connected.

246) Giving Often

Giving affects not only the one you give to, but also you, the giver. Therefore, it's not only important how much you give, but how often. Each act of giving uplifts and purifies you a little more.

Keep a small charity box attached to the wall in a conspicuous place, and place a few coins in it every day. Keep one in your home and one in your office.

247) Lend on Me

When you give for a worthy cause, it is really only a loan and G-d Himself is the guarantor. Furthermore, G_d says, the more you give, the more you get.

He's not joking. Test it and see for yourself.

248) Do Something

Perhaps the Rebbe's most common words:

The main thing is: do something!

BETWEEN WOMAN AND MAN

When the Rebbe first came to America and began to work for his father-in-law, the previous rebbe, he was put in charge of the girls' school. Since then, he always showed a sensitivity to women's issues, especially education. Publications for children had to have as many pictures of girls as boys, and any new campaign had to include women as much as men.

The Rebbe gave many public talks addressed to women only, but much of the following is taken from letters of the Rebbe to couples with marital difficulties—one of the largest categories of the Rebbe's letters. There is an awesome beauty in those letters and talks, as the Rebbe synchronizes profound mysticism with practical, workable advice.

249) Female Redeeming Power

When you look carefully into the story of the exodus, you see that the true redeeming force was the faith of the women. Today, history is repeating itself.

250) Distinctions

When G-d made the world He gave each creature, each nation and each individual a role and a meaning.

When each plays its part there is harmony.

When the lines become too blurred, there is acrimony.

251) Roles

A metaphor of the Talmud:

A man works in the field and brings home wheat—but shall he then eat wheat? Of what use is his toil?

His wife grinds the wheat into flour and makes bread.

So too, the tasks of life:

A man's spiritual accomplishments only become realized in the material world due to his wife.

252) The Female Home

G-d formed Man, but He built Woman.

She is the framework of the home in which he lives, the ground on which he builds, his walls and windows upon the world and the roof that stands over his head.

She is the crown that sets him to rule over his world.

Without woman, there is no man.

253) Two Masters

A body has two masters,
a brain and a heart.

When they work together,
each in appreciation of the other,
 the body is at harmony.

So too, Man and Woman.

254) Dividing the Chores

Changing the world is a twofold task.

Bringing spirituality into the world is principally the man's task. Elevating the world to become spiritual is principally the woman's task.

Men, generally, are meant to deal with the present. The future—and those who will live within it—is in the hands of the women.

255) Parental Guidance

From your father you may learn the things you must do. From your mother you learn who you are.

256) Disagreement

You write that you and your spouse always seem to disagree on every issue. But this is the natural way we were created. We all have our own minds. It's alright to disagree. Now you must learn to give in.

257) Unfinished Business

You complain that peace in the home is, for you, wrought with obstacles.

All of us today are souls that have been here before. In general, we return on unfinished business. Certainly, we are all responsible for doing all the good we can, and avoiding everything harmful. But that certain unfinished business, that is where the most obstacles shall be.

And those obstacles will be your only clue as to what business you are here to finish.

258) Peace at Home

The relation of husband and wife is the way our world reflects the relationship of the Creator with His Creation. There is nothing more pivotal to the world's ultimate fulfillment than this.

Therefore, as the world nears closer and closer to its fulfillment, the resistance grows stronger and stronger. By now, absolutely everything appears to be undermining the most crucial key of peace between man and woman.

259) Marriage as Microcosm

Marriage is a microcosm
of the soul's descent into this world:

If you are here looking for what you can get out of this world, then the world and all its trappings will only drag you down.

But if you are looking for what you can give, then you, your part of the world, and your soul
all are uplifted and filled with light.

So too, when you enter a marriage:
Look for what you can give, and reap harmony and love.

260) Marital Strife

When you can give in, give in. And on those matters that you cannot concede—avoid making a major issue out of them. Be pliant in the wind like a reed, and not hard and brittle like a cedar.

When your spouse will see you are not interested in making battle, but return bullets with flowers, cannon fire with sweetness, slowly, slowly the warfare will let up and you'll be able to sit and amicably work out the real issues.

261) Unconditional Love

Even if all your complaints about your spouse are well founded and valid—show her your love, nevertheless. Show her unconditional love.

It is said that all our exile is due to the sin of unmitigated hatred. When each one of us will start with unmitigated love in our own domain, from there it will spread to all else that we do, and from there to the entire world, speedily in our days, amen.

262) Conceding

Women have a greater sensitivity to emotional issues than men. So, when there is a quarrel, generally it is the man's job to concede to his wife.

263) A Good Wife

A good wife is one who
makes her husband want the right things.

264) Marital Blessing

The blessings a man receives, according to our sages, are not for himself, but for his wife and on her account.
And so, they said,
"Honor your wife so you may become wealthy."

265) Marital Peace

Nothing is greater than peace. Even when you are 100% right, and you know your spouse is 100% wrong,
you can still give in for the sake of peace.

Better a difficult peace than an easy quarrel.

CHILDREN

The Rebbe, sadly, never had any children. Yet they were so important to him. To the Rebbe, children were important not just for what they would become, but also for what they are in the present tense. He ascribed to their prayers and their good deeds tremendous power, much more than the power of adults.

The child he saw as a lucid, glistening crystal vessel in which to find G-d. More than once the Rebbe pointed out how his own thoughts strove to attain the simplicity of those of a child. In that simplicity, he taught, can be found the simplicity of the Infinite.

266) Early Impressions

Give a child kind, non-predatory stuffed animals to play with, like sheep, deer, giraffe and such. What the child looks at in those delicate years has a permanent affect.

And earlier still: Life starts in the womb. Sing to the fetus good things and speak to it kind words.

267) Punishment

Sometimes you don't know whether to punish a child or hug him. If you punish him when he needed a hug, you've made a serious mistake. But if you hug him when perhaps he should have been punished, you've just brought some extra love into the world.

268) Parental Behavior

A married couple asked for a blessing that their children behave properly. The Rebbe's reply seems simple, but since I have not seen it in any parenting book I'm including it here. Sometimes the most obvious is also the most inconvenient—and therefore the most avoided:

Behave properly yourselves. When the children see your example, they will naturally want to do the same as their parents. Then it is only a matter of talking with them, step by step, day after day, and eventually it will help.

269) Family Ties

In many ways, a family is a single organism, for in truth the child has never left the parent. When a parent's inner convictions strengthen, the child grows as well. When a child changes paths for the good, the parents feel their lives also transformed.

270) Many Children

Until recently, it was always considered the greatest of blessings to have many children.

Wealth is not a mansion filled with silver and gold. Wealth is children and grandchildren growing up on the right path.

271) All For Your Children

Every day, take one half hour to think about your children and where they're headed. Then do all you can about it. Then do more.

ALL NOAH'S CHILDREN

Over history, mankind has moved away from authority and towards the individual. But what is the religion of the individual? Some say it is humanism—the belief that all things are defined by the human mind. Accordingly, the canon goes, if human intellect will reign, all good will follow.

It confuses me, because I thought my own generation had rejected this worship of the human mind in the turmoil of the sixties, yet it lives on in so many incarnations.

Inside many of the Rebbe's teachings is a working-through of the conflict of humanism and religion, with a conclusion I can only call "post-humanism."

In other words, not stepping backwards to reject where we've come until now, but going beyond, into a mode by which our planet can sustain a future.

272) Absolute Values

For mankind to exist in harmony, we must listen to the voice that Noah heard after the flood.

We must accept that there is a set of absolute values set by the Creator of the world, values that cannot be played about with to suit our convenience.

Values from beyond the subjective minds of men.

273) Beyond Humanism

People call me "old-fashioned" for my belief in an ancient and timeless teaching and for my faith in G-d.
In truth, it is they who are old-fashioned,
for they cling to an idea that failed decades ago.

The Age of Reason, of Enlightenment, of Humanism—when Knowledge and Intellect were worshipped as the Redeemers of Mankind—all this died and was buried when the most civilized and intellectual nation on earth committed the most unthinkable atrocities.

Man, *to survive*, must accept, feel, stand in awe and connect to That Which Is Above Him.

274) Fighting Crime

If you tell a child, "Keep this rule because if you don't you will be punished!" the child has two doubts in his mind: Maybe he won't be caught, and if he is caught, maybe the punishment won't outweigh the crime.

The child has to know that there is an eye that sees, an ear that hears—that there is a Higher Unseen Being to which he is answerable. This is the only way to reduce crime in America.

275) The Sterile Classroom

In our zeal to separate church and state, we have effectively removed any concept of the supernal or the spiritual from the classroom.

A child grows up today learning about a face-value world centered around his own self. There is no awe.

276) Warning

I was there in Germany before the war, and I tell you, the same thing could happen here in America
if the subject of morality is not allowed to enter
the public schools.

277) Distributing Truth

Before, there was a hierarchy of truth. The high priest of Egypt had the real truth. The scribes had secrets of the truth. Their initiated students had inklings. The people wallowed in ignorance.

Moses, the revolutionary, changed all that. At Mount Sinai, all men, women and children, princes and commoners, priests and workers, had to be present. All received the same truth, all at once. Even the priestly rites were made public knowledge.

Before, power and authority was based on withholding knowledge. In a Torah world, authority is established through universal knowledge.

278) Dawn of a New Age

At the time of the disarmament talks in the U.N. (January 1992):

On the wall outside the United Nations building,
the nations of the world have inscribed their goal,
the words of the Prophet Isaiah,

"They shall beat their swords into plough shares
and their spears into pruning forks."

Now the Cold War has ended and funds for arms will go instead to feed empty stomachs. Armies will be used to bring food to strangers. The prophecy has begun to be realized.

But the Cold War did not end due to Man's power of reason. War never made sense—yet the same rational Man has fought them for millennium.
All that is new is that the light of a new age has begun to shine in our world.

THE BLUEPRINT OF CREATION

The Rebbe's principal activity was studying—pouring over the texts of the Talmud, the legal codes and responsa, Kabbalah and philosophy—every aspect of the wealth of Torah, examining and comparing from every angle, asking the questions others were afraid to ask and providing solutions nobody thought to answer.

True, he was running an international activist organization with hundreds of offices across the globe. True, he received bags of mail every day. True, he himself was the one who demanded action and not just ideas. Yet his principal occupation—what he spoke about, what he wrote about, how he spent most of the hours of his day—was Torah study.

The Rebbe often repeated that through the study of Torah you could conquer the world. And from the way the Rebbe discussed Torah you could see he was doing just that: Every thought, every teaching was a new understanding of the entire universe. A simple story or a seemingly dry legalistic point became in his hands an insight to the workings of time and space.

In fact, spending that degree of time on study is a strong statement in itself. It says, "This of me that you see involved in the world and its affairs, this is not me—this is a mere glimmer of my soul.

Where I truly am is in an intimate union with a G‑dly teaching that is beyond time and beyond the whole creation."

Only one who is firmly anchored in a higher realm can effect true change within our world.

279) Instructions

They translate it as "The Bible", or "The Law", but that's not what the word means. Torah means "instructions." Whatever piece of Torah you learn, you *must* find the instructions it is giving you.

280) Blueprint

Torah is the blueprint by which the world was designed. Everything that exists can be found in the Torah. Even more: In any one concept of Torah you can find the entire world.

281) Penetrating Wisdom

At Mount Sinai, tradition tells, there was no echo.

Torah penetrates and is absorbed by all things, because it is their essence. There is no place where it does not apply, no darkness it does not illuminate, nothing it cannot bring alive. Nothing will bounce it back and say, "Torah is too holy to belong here."

282) Multiple Reflections

Go out on a clear night and see the moon reflected in the water of a lake. Then see the very same moon reflected in a pond, in a teacup, in a single drop of water.

So the same essential Torah is reflected within each person who studies it, from a small child to a great sage.

283) Where Lives the Torah

Where is the Torah? Does it reside in the heavens with the angels? Or in a parchment scroll in the ark of the synagogue? Or with the rabbis and scholars?

It lives in the heart of each person who learns it, in the voice of the one who discusses it and in the life of the one who lives it.

That heart, that voice, that life, that, too, is G-d's word.

284) Become Truth

There is no truth about G-d.

Truth *is* G-d.

There is no one who learns Truth.

You *become* Truth.

There is no need to search for Truth.

You have inherited it and it is within you.

You need only learn quietness

to listen to that inheritance.

285) Post-Sinai

Before Mount Sinai, there was earth and there was heaven. If you wanted one, you were obliged to abandon the other.

At Sinai, the boundaries of heaven and earth were breached and Man was empowered to fuse the two: To raise the earthly into the realm of the spirit, and to bring heaven down to earth.

Before Mount Sinai, the coarse material of which the world is made could not be elevated. It could be used as a medium, an aid in achieving enlightenment, but it itself could not be enlightened. The spirit was raised, but the earth remained dark.

At Sinai we were empowered to take physical objects and transform it them into spiritual artifacts.

Our forefathers' task was to enlighten the souls of men. Ours is to transform the material darkness into light.

286) More Than Stories

People think the Torah is all about laws and customs and quaint stories, with a mystical side as well.

In truth, the Torah is entirely spiritual. But when you cannot perceive the spiritual, all you see are laws and quaint stories.

287) Mystical & Practical

You cannot separate the mystical from the practical. Each thing has both a body and a soul, and they act as one. Neither can contradict the other, and in each the other can be found.

288) Start Simple

If you want to understand something to its depths, first approach it with the mind of a five year old.

Ask the innocent and obvious questions and make things clear and simple. Through that clarity, you will perceive the depths.

289) Wonder

Amazement never ceases for the enlightened mind.

At every moment it views with amazement the wonder of an entire world renewed out of the void, and asks, "Why is there anything at all and not just nothing?"

290) Fool With Answers

One who has all the answers is less than a fool.

A fool at least asks a question.

291) Wisdom & the Rebel

The rebel is far closer to wisdom than the complacent child—as an ox is more powerful than a lamb. He only needs a wise person who can show him how to harness his strength and bring much good to the world.

292) Questions

Questions are also part of the truth.

293) Gradual Truth

In life, you don't get all the answers at once.

First you must absorb and live with one simple truth. Then later you must find another truth—one that may seem to conflict with and negate all you previously learned. Then, from that confusion, emerges a higher truth—the inner light behind all you had learned before.

294) Forgetting to Learn

Learning is not the mere acquisition of knowledge and more knowledge. Learning is a process of making quantum leaps beyond the subjective self. No matter how high a summit you may reach, there is always another peak above.

But you can only reach that peak once you realize you are still in the valley.

The Talmud tells of Rabbi Zera, who fasted one hundred fasts to forget all the Torah he had learned in Babylonia before going to study the Torah of the land of Israel.

295) Inner Study

You may ask, "Why must I study and learn?
Is not the truth already within me?"

The truth is locked within you, deep in slumber.
It is awakened and liberated by the truth that comes from without.

296) Meditation

This is what meditation is: Once you have thoroughly learned a concept and organized the ideas in your mind you then try to visualize it. Once you have visualization, you try to feel the essential life of the thing.

If your mind is completely focused, then the idea will move you until you are no longer the same self
and your day is no longer the same day.
Then it has become yours.

297) Owning Wisdom

You can live in a palace filled with treasures and still be poor. To be wealthy you must *own* the things you have.

So too with poverty of the mind: You may have all the knowledge and brilliant ideas in the world, but you are still poor until they have become part of you.

298) Morning Meditation

When you get up in the morning, let the world wait. Defy it a little. First learn something to inspire you.
Take a few moments to meditate upon it.

And then you may plunge ahead into the darkness,
full of light with which to illuminate it.

299) Real Ideas

I don't believe in philosophy.

I believe in ideas that change people.

300) Change By Doing

People are not changed by arguments, nor by philosophy. People are changed by *doing*.

Introduce a new habit into your life, and your entire perspective of the world changes.

First *do*, then learn about what you are already doing.

301) Sun & Moon

Every created being is both the sun and the moon.

The sun gives constantly of its warmth and its light.
The moon, on the other hand, only reflects the light it receives from the sun.

So too, there is nothing in G-d's world that may only take without giving. Each thing has something unique to offer—for otherwise it would never have been created. And there is nothing that may give without receiving.

Every created being must both give and receive,
be the sun as well as the moon.

302) Sun & Moon II

Each one of us is both the sun and the moon.

The sun is constant—every day the same fiery ball rises in the sky. But the moon cycles through constant change—one day it is whole, then it wanes until it has disappeared all together. Yet, then it is renewed, reborn out of nothingness.

So too, we learn and progress by quantum leaps and bounds, yet the timeless, constant wisdom of Torah doesn't budge from its place. On the contrary, the more we move forward, the deeper we fathom the truths behind us.

303) Teacher

A student begins as a sponge or as a funnel:
Either everything is absorbed, indiscriminately
—or everything passes in one ear and out the other.

The first job of a teacher, therefore, is to direct the student and tell him, "Focus on this, this is important.
Do not focus on this—this is only the background."

304) Fill Your House

A container is defined by its contents: A pitcher of water is water. A crate of apples is apples. A house, too, is defined by what it contains.

Fill your house with books of Torah, and your house becomes a Torah. Affix charity boxes to its walls, and your house becomes a wellspring of charity. Bring those who need a warm home to your table, and your house becomes a lamp in the darkness.

305) Fixed Time

If you're serious about something, it has a fixed time. If you're earnest about getting something done and the phone rings, you ignore it.

The spiritual side of your life is not a hobby, nor a luxury—it is your purpose of existence. When you are learning Torah, or meditating or in prayer, nothing else exists.

Your spiritual career should have *at least* equal priority to your worldly career.

FAITH & INTELLECT

They say someone asked the Rebbe's wife what she thought of her husband. "I'll tell you one thing," she replied. "My husband believes in G‑d."

Great faith of a simple mind is not so impressive. Simple faith of a great mind is. Perhaps the simple person just hasn't asked the right questions. Perhaps faith is convenient for him. Perhaps he's afraid of what his wife might do to him if he came home one day and announced he no longer believes.

A truly great mind is not swayed by such concerns. Nothing forces him to believe—he believes because it is the truth. And since his faith is not self-serving, but founded on a truth beyond the self, therefore it is absolute; it is unshakable, down to the detail. And very infectious.

306) Belief

From a letter:

You write to me you are concerned that you don't believe. If you don't believe, then why does not believing concern you?

307) True Belief

From another letter:

I do not accept your assertion that you do not believe. For if you truly had no concept of a Supernal Being Who created the world with purpose, then what is all this outrage of yours against the injustice of life? The substance of the universe is not moral, nor are the plants and animals. Why should it surprise you that whoever is bigger and more powerful swallows his fellow alive?

It is only due to an inner conviction in our hearts, shared by every human being, that there is a Judge, that there is right and there is wrong. And so, when we see a wrong, we demand an explanation: Why is this not the way it is supposed to be?

That itself is belief in G-d.

308) Higher Faith

There is sub-rational faith—faith in dogma. Then there is super-rational faith—intuitive knowledge, consciousness of a higher reality, a glimmer of the infinite within the finite human being.

309) Inherited Faith

Our job is not to *have* faith. We have faith already, whether we want it or not. It comes in our blood from our ancestors who gave their lives for it. Our job is to transport that higher vision that gave them their faith down into our minds, into our personalities, into our words, into our actions in daily life. To make it part of our selves and our world.

310) Beyond Intellect

Your mind itself no more than a creation, a whim of a Creator who fashioned it from nothing.

To approach the One Who Created Intellect, you need a sense which is beyond intellect and beyond self. We call this sense אמונה—emunah, which some translate as faith.

But this type of faith does not ignore intellect.
It takes you far beyond.

311) Understanding Wonder

That there are matters we don't understand is obvious—how could the finite intellect of an inherently subjective mortal being, imprisoned within the confines of time and space, be expected to fathom the infinite wisdom of
the Creator?

The great wonder is that there are matters
we *can* understand.

312) Ultimate Knowledge

Any reason we may suppose for G-d's will could not be the ultimate reason. The finite mind cannot begin to fathom an infinite wisdom—never mind that which brought forth wisdom from the Void.

The ultimate knowledge is that we do not know.

313) Beyond Understanding

G-d knows all before it occurs. More than that: It is His knowledge that brings all events into being.

But we still have free choice.

You claim this is illogical. I ask you: Knowledge of existence before any thought of any thing exists *is* logical?

When we talk about the Source of All Existence, our principles of logic no longer apply. We don't understand a thing, because there is no understanding.

314) Omniscience and Free Choice

There are those who are unable to proceed with life because they have concluded that everything is just fate. We are always thinking in terms of a cause and an effect, that there is a world which is being directed and a G-d that directs it. Therefore, we imagine there is no room for free choice—since He calls all the shots.

But for Him there is no such dynamic. There is no cause because there is nothing to cause, no effect because there is only Him. Whatever happens is Him and our free choice is also Him.

In our world there is free choice. In His, there is only Him. You continue living in your world and leave His up to Him.

315) A Little Smarter

If G-d were only a little smarter than me,
He wouldn't be my G-d.

316) Reason & Faith

Don't imagine that you can escape faith. Every science, every system of logic, has its axioms. Reason cannot move one step forward without some assumption upon which to base itself.

317) Insufficient Understanding

Let's say you saw a magnificent machine, with hundreds of thousands of parts, all working in spectacular unison and harmony, far beyond anything the human mind could contrive. And you examined the details of this machine and found that some aspects of its workings puzzle you. Would you complain to the inventor? Or would you pray in awe for understanding?

In general, the universe's wondrous design is obvious. We just have to admit insufficient understanding of certain aspects.

318) Complacent

The Rebbe spoke about the suffering in the world, and when he came to these words, began to choke and sob:

If He is truly capable of anything,
then why can't He provide good without the bad?

And if His Torah contains the answers for all questions, why does it not answer this one?

There could be only one answer:

He does not wish us to know,
because if we knew
we might consent.

319) Questioning the Divine

To Elie Wiesel:

Abraham, father of us all, questioned G-d's justice. So did Moses. So did Akiva. So did many enlightened souls. You are not the first.

Of all those who questioned, there were two approaches: Those who meant it, and those who did not.

Those who wanted understanding gained understanding—a sense of nothingness encountering a reality far beyond our puny minds.

Those who asked but did not want to understand gained nothing.

320) After the Holocaust

Elie Wiesel asked the Rebbe,

"How can you believe in G-d after the holocaust?"

The Rebbe asked Elie Wiesel,

"How can you not believe in G-d after the holocaust?"

Last I heard, Elie Wiesel was believing.

321) How Could It Happen

You ask me, "Why did G-d allow it to happen?"

You recognize that everything in this world has purpose and meaning. Examine any aspect of His vast Creation, from the cosmos to the workings of the atom and you will see there *must* be a plan.

And so you ask, where does *this* fit into the plan?
How could it?

I can only answer, painfully, G-d alone knows.

But what I cannot know, I need not know.

I need not know in order to fulfill
that which my Creator has created me to do.

And that is, to change the world
so this could never happen again.

322) Objective Faith

If your belief system is based upon what makes sense to you, what you find most gratifying and what best accommodates your own self-concept—then you will undoubtedly fear intellectual inquiry. At best, your approach will be subjective and bribed.

However, when your faith is based not upon your subjective self, but because this is the reality of your inner soul, a truth to which it is intrinsically bound—then you are not afraid to inquire. There is no apprehension of being proven wrong, only certitude that you shall understand more.

Therefore, only true faith can be truly objective.

323) Cold Intellect

There is a cold, harsh land where G-dliness is not allowed to come, and it is called Intellect. As the Zohar says, "Intellect cannot grasp Him at all."

Yet, ultimately, G-dliness must come to dwell even in that place which by definition cannot contain Him. Your mind must struggle to understand all that it can, and then even harder to sense that which cannot be known.

324) Two Are One

Many people, without realizing, end up with two gods:

One god is an impersonal one, an all-encompassing, transcendent force.

But then, at times of trouble, they cry out to another, personal god, with whom they have an intimate relationship.

Our faith is all about knowing that these two are one. The same G-d who is beyond all things, He is the same one who hears your cries and counts your tears. The same G-d that is the force behind all existence and transcends even that, He is the same G-d who cares about what is cooking in your kitchen and how you treat your fellow man.

G-d cannot be defined, even as transcendent. He is beyond all things and within them at once.

325) Faith & Experience

Faith is not the result of experience.

On the contrary, faith is an act that comes from within and *creates* experience.

Things happen because you trust they will.

326) Belief & Trust

Belief is not enough—you need Trust.

A believer can be a thief and a murderer.

Trust in G-d changes the way you live.

327) American Money

Do you know why American money is so successful? Because it has written on it, "In G-d We Trust."
Not just *"Believe." "Trust."*

Furthermore, the money even tells you its purpose: Upon it is written, "E Pluribus Unum." The purpose of all your dealings with money is to make from many a Oneness. And if that is truly your purpose, then you will rely on the One Creator to provide your needs.

328) Life That Works

We have found a way of life that works.
We have 3300 years of testing under every possible condition to prove that.

Yes, you could hold off until you've tested all possible modes of life, made comparisons and come to your own conclusions.
But what a waste of precious time it will be—for yourself and for the world that could be benefiting from you. After all, how much life will you have left after reaching your conclusions?

329) Time Out

From a letter:

You write that you have taken a few years off from teaching to come to an understanding of
"what it is all about."

Tell me, once you have determined an answer to your question, what will you do then?
And in the meantime, just who and how many have benefited from all your searching?

Go back to teaching and search there while you change a few students' lives.

330) Proof

In life, we almost never wait for 100% guarantees. We trust that the dentist is a dentist, the taxi driver is a taxi driver, and so on—and put our lives in their hands—on flimsy tacit evidence.

Yet, when it comes to a simple good deed, people demand 100% proof that this is really what G-d wants them to do!

SCIENCE AND TECHNOLOGY

The Rebbe studied both sciences and humanities at the University of Berlin and at the Sorbonne.

Throughout the nineteenth century and for most of the twentieth, rabbis dealt with the "challenge of science." Generally, their approach was the classic one of apologetics, redefining tradition so it would not conflict with what science seemed to say.

The Rebbe was intolerant of such apologetics. To him there was no conflict to begin with, only a gross misunderstanding of what science is and what it says.

331) Einstein's G-d

Einstein received acclaim for demonstrating that energy and matter are one. The scientist who demonstrates how *all* forces are one in a unified theory will receive even greater acclaim.

So, since we all agree that someone will eventually establish this, why not accept it right now, and we'll call it G-d?

332) Science & G-d

In the nineteenth century, many scientists had no use for G-d. Instead, they worshipped a tight chain of cause and effect that left no room for miracles, providence or prophecy.

But then the scientist looked into the atom and the wonder of the universe opened before him. The iron chain of cause and effect was loosened and Determinism deposed from its throne. Today, once again there is room for G-d in the minds of men.

333) Discoveries & Inventions

Everything was created as a means to know G-d.

Every discovery we have ever made, each of our inventions, was planted here in the six days of creation in order that we utilize it for a G-dly purpose.

334) Life on Mars

A young biologist was working at NASA on a project to find life on Mars. He asked the Rebbe, "Is this okay? Some religions say we shouldn't search. After all, the Bible doesn't say anything about life on Mars."

The Rebbe replied, "Professor Green, you should look for life on Mars. And if you don't find it there, you should look elsewhere. Because for you to sit here and say that G-d didn't create life elsewhere is to put limits on G-d, and no one can do that."

335) Scientific Revolution

Over 1700 years in advance, the author of the Zohar predicted a revolution of science and technology beginning in the middle of the last century. There he describes the fountains of wisdom bursting forth from the ground and flooding the earth—all in preparation for an era when the world shall be filled with wisdom and knowledge of the Oneness of its Creator.

From this we know that the true purpose of all technology and modern science is neither convenience nor power, but a means to discover G-dliness within the physical world.

336) Communication Technology

Communication technologies have provided us a metaphor to comprehend how One Being can perceive all things in a single instance.

It makes you wonder how previous generation could possibly have understood such things.

337) E=MC$_2$

Modern physics has brought us to a realization of the oneness of our universe, from which we may better grasp the Oneness of its Creator:

All that exists can be divided into two elements: The force, and the particle that bears that force. In other terms: quality and quantity. With a simple equation, Einstein demonstrated that even these two elements are truly one.

338) Science From the Top Down

The scientist's understanding begins from the outside and attempts to work in—from the bottom up. He begins with subjective empiricism and attempts to deduce an objective model.

The wisdom of Torah begins from the inside and works its way out—from the top down. In this approach you meditate upon the Creator's own objective model and apply it to discover the truth behind this world.

The prudent scientist will realize that he can benefit most through a combination of both approaches.

339) Gravity

No one has ever seen, touched or measured a particle or a wave of gravity. Furthermore, the very notion of gravity is mystifying: Masses light years apart with nothing between them, affecting each other's movements!

Yet we all accept there must be a cause behind the phenomena we observe, so we call this elusive force "gravity."

So too, there is a cause behind existence. That Cause may be even more elusive, but the reality of its existence is at least as inescapable and empirically evident.

MY PEOPLE

People want to know how the Rebbe attracted so many admirers. It's really quite a simple formula:

Many became leaders because they brought their people to believe in them. The Rebbe was a great leader because he believed so much in his people.

340) The Master's Prayer

The enlightened master knows he lacks nothing
and so he prays for his people.

But if he knows he lacks nothing,
then he knows that in truth they also lack nothing,
and if so, for what is he praying?

He prays they should have open eyes to see
and open hearts to know
that in truth they lack nothing.

But how can one who lacks nothing pray?

Because he knows he himself lacks nothing,
but deeper, at his very core,
he is his people
and he prays as one of them.

341) Three Loves

When the Rebbe accepted the mantle of leadership, this was his acceptance speech:

If you find a Jew who has love of G-d, but lacks love of his people and love of Torah, tell him that this love cannot last.

If you find a Jew who has love of his people, but lacks love of G-d and love of Torah, work with him to nurture this love until it overflows into the other two, until all three join in one tight knot that will never be untied.

342) Heart of the World

Hormones, vitamins, chromosomes, etc., make up only a minuscule portion of the body—yet they are the most crucial elements of life.

Jews are the smallest minority of all the peoples of the world—yet they are the most vital element of history.

They are the heart of the world.
If they are healthy, the world is healthy.

343) Without Distinction

To a rabbi who wrote about "secular Jews":

You categorize them as religious Jews and secular Jews. How do you make such a distinction?

There is no such thing as a secular Jew! All of them are holy.

344) Four Sons

The Torah speaks about four sons. One wise, one wicked, one in a state of wonder, one who does not realize he should ask.

What do they all have in common?

"One."

As in, "Hear O Israel, G-d our Lord, G-d is One."

That "One" is the essence of every Jew
—even the one the Torah calls "wicked."

345) Heretics

There are no heretics nowadays.

You have to know an awful lot to be a heretic.

346) Living Jews

At the onset of the Persian Gulf crisis, a certain prominent rabbi in Israel was preaching that the Jews were about to be punished for the sinners amongst them. They told me they had never seen the Rebbe angry before:

The sages tell us that our father Jacob never died. "Since his children are alive, he is alive."

Each and every Jew is the personification of his father Jacob, and the heart of each and every Jew is alive and beating strong. To say about any one of them that he is spiritually dead is to pronounce our father Jacob dead. If to you it appears that way, the fault is in you, not in the Jew you observe.

G-d sees only good in them. He will make great miracles for them and they will be safe.

347) We Are One

The Jewish people are one.

A Jew putting on tefillin in America affects the safety of a Jewish soldier in Israel.

348) Each One's Mitzvah

Every Jew has a mitzvah to which he finds an affinity. Don't argue with him. Find that mitzvah and encourage him in it.

349) Inseparable Souls

It is our nature that each one of us finds it impossible to knowingly separate himself from our G-d.

350) Never Distant

After many years, some began to follow the Rebbe's lead and reach out to Jews who were not living a traditional Jewish life. They called it, "Bringing close those who are distant." The term did not find favor in the Rebbe's eyes. He wrote:

You say you are "bringing close those who are distant"?! What gives you the right to call them distant and pretend you are close? You must approach each one as though you were an emissary sent by the King of kings of kings to talk with the prince, his only son!

DAYS ARE COMING…

It is an ancient tradition that in every generation there is one above all others who is the heart of all those alive on the face of the earth. When one passes on, another takes over.

This is my gut feeling: The Rebbe was the heart of the Boomers and of all those born in their wake.

Then, sometimes, I look at the face of the Rebbe, and I think, "This, my heart? But we are so distant! His world, my world…I am he and he is me?! If he is my own heart, then how do I feel such a stranger to him?!"

But then, do you feel your heart beating within you? Most people will answer they don't and cannot, unless they search for a pulse somewhere. But isn't that absurd: Your entire body is incessantly throbbing in every limb and organ with the relentless pumping of the heart—and you say you do not feel it? It is just that it is so close to you, so much you, that you cannot feel it, just as you do not notice your own nose in front of you.

All events of body and mind reflect the nuances of the beating of the heart and of the life-giving blood that passes through it.

All our searching for higher fulfillment, all our rejection of the established order, all our awaiting of "the Aquarian Age" or "the New Age" or whatever you want to call it—all is an expression of the consciousness that flows to us, pumped through the heart of our generation.

351) Time Line

1951: We are the last generation of the exile and the first of a new age.

1967: A mighty wind of return is blowing. I hear the sound of a great ram's horn. The souls of the young people are preparing for a time to come.

1990: The time line of Mankind, according to tradition, is divided into six millennium corresponding to the six days of Creation. The seventh millennium is beyond time.

According to this paradigm, the year 5751 (October 1990–September 1991) equates with high noon on the sixth day.

The year 5751 begins an entirely new era. Just as on Friday afternoon we begin the mad rush to prepare for the seventh day, so too all the wonders you will see in this year are nature's frenzy to prepare for a time beyond time. We are about to enter what the ancient sages referred to as the Era of Moshiach.

352) One Last Adjustment

Our deeds are but catalysts to change the world. Their size and visible impact are not what really matters.

In everything you do, consider that there is but one last fine adjustment the world needs before it may transform. Who knows—perhaps this one is it.

353) Nothing to Fear

There are some who are afraid of a new age.
They wonder, "What will happen to my career?
My whole lifestyle will have to change!
What about all the acquaintances and connections I've spent a lifetime building? And what about all my worldly possessions, my retirement plan, my investments? Will they take my car away?"

Even these people have nothing to fear.
The era that is coming is not something separate from our times. It is pieced together from everything we do now, and all that we know of shall remain. Only the negativity will vanish, and the G-dliness within each thing will be obvious for us to see.

354) Distortion Removal

The material world is a place where each thing seems to say, "Here I am and here I always was."—as though it has no source.

In fact, only the Essence of All Things has no source. He was and is and always will be. This is the truth of what our world is trying to tell us: It is only trying to express—in a distorted way—its own true essence, the Essence of All Things that has no source. But a time will be when the distortion shall vanish and we shall see nothing but that Essence.

355) Darkness Limited

Everything has its limits, even darkness.

As the Zohar says,
"When the world was made, a limit was set
how long it will function in confusion."

356) Spring

We are not waiting for some great revelation from above to save us from our incompetence as guardians of this world and put everything in order. Rather, we are waiting to see the sun rise over everything we have done, to see the fruits of our labors blossom in an eternal spring.

It will come upon the world as a spring rain upon a plowed and seeded field. Plow and sow now, while there is still time.

357) Where Will I Be?

It will happen with you or without you, whether you believe in it or not. True, you could help it be sooner. But the fact is, it will be in our times whether you help or not. And it will be good for you, no matter what.

But have you asked yourself, "Where will I be standing when that time comes? What will I be involved in? Will I be part of it, or will it be despite me?"

358) Defiant Darkness

People ask, "But how could you see so much good in the future when so much evil predominates now—and it grows day by day?"

But such is the order of things: Darkness was only placed in the world to challenge light. As the light intensifies, the darkness thickens to defy it.

359) Before Dawn

They say the most profound darkness comes just before the dawn. The harshest oppression of our forefathers in Egypt came just before their liberation.

That was a coarse darkness of slavery of the body. Today it is a darkness of the soul, a deep slumber of the spirit of Man. There are sparks of light, glimmerings of a sun that never shone before—but the darkness of night overwhelms all.

Prepare for dawn.

360) Silence Before the Flood

A parable:

A father answers the questions of his child and they are happy together, in joyful dialogue.

Then the child asks a question, and the father must think deeply—not just for the answer, but to reach to the essence of this answer so he may bring it to the world of his child. For a long while, the father is quiet.

And so, the child becomes anxious and begins to cry. "Father, where are you? Why do you no longer talk to me? Why have you deserted me for your own thoughts?"

And then the father begins to speak, but this time it is the deepest core of his mind that surges into the mind and heart of the child. A surging current of such power that with this, the child, too, may become a father.

The child is us. The time of silence is now.

When the spirit of Man is dark, when the flow gates of Above seem all but sealed, prepare for liberation.

361) The Dream

You build a dream house.

You start with a dream. The dream becomes a plan. The plan becomes a lot of dirty work. The dirty work becomes a house.

If you are successful, it is the house of your dreams.

Dream, plan, dirty work, success. Why is this the fundamental strategy of all human endeavor? Because it is the story of the universe.

Those who can feel the dream, those who can read the plan, they see we are now at the finishing touches.

362) Retroactive Liberation

Before I had even started school, a picture of liberation was already forming in my mind. Such a liberation, and in such a way, that it shall truly make sense of all the suffering, all the oppression and persecution we have undergone.

It is not that there will be no more darkness, no more suffering, that those things shall cease to exist. It will be such an essence-light that darkness itself will become light—*even the darkness and suffering of the past.*

363) Wellsprings

There is a story that tells it all. On the awesome day of Rosh Hashana, the Jewish New Year, of the year 5507 (1746), the Baal Shem Tov lay in deep meditation and ascended to the holy chamber of the Moshiach.

"Master," he asked, "when shall you come?"

The answer: "When your wellsprings shall spread to the outside."

The wellsprings are the wellsprings of the deepest inner wisdom.

Not only the *water* of the wellsprings, but the *wellsprings* themselves must spread forth. When the furthest reaches of the material world shall become wellsprings of the innermost wisdom, then the Moshiach shall come.

This is our mandate now. Don't be satisfied with drinking from the wellsprings. Become one, wherever you are.

364) Inner Exile

It is not so much that we need to be taken out of exile.

It is that the exile must be taken out of us.

365) Open Eyes

Autumn 1991, a few months before his fatal stroke:

After 3307 years, all that's needed has been done.

The table is set, the feast of Moshiach is being served with the Ancient Wine, the Leviathan and the Wild Ox—and we are sitting at it.

All that's left is to open our eyes and see.

Those last words I write, but I do not understand. But then, if I understood them, I suppose I would not need to be told to open my eyes.

TRANSMISSION

It was a late spring evening in 1991 and the Rebbe had just returned from the gravesite of his father-in-law, the previous rebbe. He had spent the entire day there, on an almost empty stomach, reading letters and reciting psalms. Now he said the evening prayers, then turned to the people to speak. Words such as had never before been heard from his mouth.

He spoke to us about his frustration, how his goals had not been achieved. He had done everything he could to awaken the Jewish people from their slumber and complacency, that we should demand a world the way the world was meant to be, that we should want with all our hearts to break out of our spiritual prisons. But, the Rebbe lamented, it was all to no avail. The world remains within its shell, and us, its captives, still in our chains. The time of which he had always dreamt, the goal to which everything he had ever done was aimed, had not been achieved. And the Rebbe had no explanation why.

"The only thing I am able to do," the Rebbe continued, "is hand the matter over to you. Do everything you can—even if it demands the unconventional, the maverick but down-to-earth—do everything you can that people will truly yearn—not because I have told them to yearn, but because they truly yearn from their own hearts and their own understanding—and demand, 'How much longer!?'"

"If there were only a few souls, even just ten of them, that would be sincere and stubborn and demand from G‑d—we would already be there today"

"So I have done my part. From this point on, you do whatever *you* can."

But the Rebbe did not retire. On the contrary, although approaching his ninetieth year, he accelerated. Every week was another public gathering. Every Sunday, the Rebbe stood for hours, greeting visitors with blessings and advice—and a dollar to give to charity. More teachings and writings than for years before came out at that time.

But the message was clear: The torch that had been passed from leader to leader, from prophet to sage since Abraham, that torch had now been passed to each of us, to anyone who would grab it. And we are to cross the finish line.

After eleven months, the Rebbe tidied his desk, leaving there nothing but a photo album of the families of those who work for him. He travelled for the last time to the gravesite of his father-in-law, where he fell from a major stroke. Although unable to speak more than a few words, he continued providing guidance and counsel from his bed and armchair. Two years later to that very same day, the Rebbe suffered another stroke. Three months and a few days afterwards, the Rebbe passed on.

The Rebbe believed in our orphaned, post-holocaust generation. We won't let him down.

THE CREED OF NOAH

At the dawn of creation G-d gave the first human being six rules to follow in order that His world be sustained. Later, after the Great Flood, he charged Noah with one more. So it is recounted in the Book of Genesis as interpreted by our tradition in the Talmud.

For most of Jewish history, circumstance did not permit our people to promulgate these principles, other than by indirect means. When the Rebbe began speaking about publicizing them as a preparation for a new era, he was reviving an almost lost tradition.

What fascinates me is the breathing room they provide. They are like the guidelines of a great master of music or art: firm, reliable and comprehensive—but only a base, and upon this base each people and every person may build.

According to the sages of the Talmud, there are 70 families with 70 paths within the great Family of Man. And each individual has his or her path within a path. Yet there is one universal basis for us all.

Anyone who lives by these rules, acknowledging that they are what G-d wants of us, is considered by our tradition to be righteous. That person is a builder with a share in the world as it is meant to be.

Here are those seven instructions, according to ancient tradition:

I will not worship anyone or anything other than the One Creator, Who cares for the creatures of our world, renewing the Act of Creation at every moment in infinite wisdom, being life for each thing.

-

I will not show disrespect for the Creator in any way.

-

I will not murder.

-

I will respect the laws of marriage between man and woman.

-

I will not take that which does not rightfully belong to me.

-

I will not cause needless harm to any living thing.

-

I will uphold courts of truth and justice in my land.

"So I have done my part. From this point on,
you do whatever you can.

Index of Meditations

& Moses, 152

42 Journeys, 36

A Fire, 159
A Good Wife, 221
A Story, 26
Absolute Values, 228
Adam's Challenge, 115
Advice on Anger, 91
After the Holocaust, 261
All For Your Children, 226
All of You, 102
All or No One, 175
American Money, 266
Animal Taming, 92
Another Chance, 114
Anxiety, 72
As Per Design, 112
Attitude, 69
Authentic Humility, 142

Be a Miracle, 54
Be There, 36
Beauty, 64
Become Light, 30
Become Truth, 238
Before Dawn, 288
Belief, 252
Belief & Trust, 265
Believing in Good, 78
Between Hope & Trust, 96
Beyond Humanism, 229
Beyond I, 147
Beyond Intellect, 255
Beyond Reason, 209
Beyond the Darkness, 125
Beyond the Possible, 155
Beyond Understanding, 256
Bigger Than Big, 25

Birthdays, 62
Black Holes, 64
Blood Pressure, 131
Blueprint, 235

Celebrate!, 96
Change By Doing, 247
Childish Joy, 106
Choosing Life, 95
Chutzpah, 113
Cleaning Up, 87
Cold Intellect, 263
Communication Technology, 272
Complacent, 260
Conceding, 221
Confidence, 79
Confidence & Humility, 141
Congratulations, 87
Connecting, 181
Consent, 88

Darkness Limited, 286
Darkness Transformed, 126
Dawn of a New Age, 232
Defiant Darkness, 288
Delight to Anguish, 194
Denying Reality, 98
Despair on Purpose, 104
Determinism, 53
Detoured Good, 208
Dig Deeper, 195
Disagreement, 218
Discoveries & Inventions, 271
Distinctions, 215
Distortion Removal, 286
Distributing Truth, 231
Dividing the Chores, 217
Do, 72
Do Something, 212
Doctor & Friend, 131

Down To Earth, 20
Dream, 290

E=MC$_2$, 273
Each Day, 37
Each One's Mitzvah, 280
Early Impressions, 224
Earthly Truth, 174
Ego Activist, 191
Ego Dieting, 154
Einstein's G-d, 270
Electricity, 63
Escape, 149
Essence Garden, 24
Essential Peace, 28
Every Detail, 34
Everything!, 106
Excuses, 117
Exploiting the Darkness, 125

Failure, 123
Faith, 259
Faith & Experience, 265
Family Ties, 225
Fear, 116
Female Redeeming Power, 214
Fighting Crime, 229
Fill Your House, 250
Fixed Time, 250
Focus, 105
Following Advice, 77
Fool With Answers, 242
Fools, 164
Forgetting to Learn, 244
Four Realms, 149
Four Sons, 278
Four Steps, 133
Fragments, 184
Free Love, 156
Friendly Hardships, 112
From the Core, 124
Functional Light, 32
Fur Coats and Fireplaces, 150

G-d in Exile, 161

G-d Involved, 46
G-d's Plea, 23
Getting Out of the Way, 80
Givers & Takers, 206
Giving Often, 211
Going Over, 110
Gradual Truth, 244
Gratefulness, 107
Gravity, 274

Handshake, 184
Harmony, 80
Healthy Body, Healthy Soul, 130
Heart of the World, 277
Heaven, 178
Hell, 178
Helpful Knowledge, 195
Helping, 193
Heretics, 279
High Souls, 180
Higher & Closer, 99
Higher & Higher, 209
Higher Faith, 254
Higher Lower, 24
Higher Reality, 44
Higher Truth, 165
Home, 21
Hope, 90
How Could It Happen, 262
Howard Hughes, 59
Humble Compassion, 207
Humble Joy, 101
Hypocrisy, 188

Imagining, 45
Impact, 103
Impossible, 49
In All Ways, 107
In Case of Doubt, 132
In Sum, 84
In Trouble Together, 186
Inferiority, 116
Infinite Opportunity, 210
Inherited Faith, 254

Inner Exile, 292
Inner Peace, 171
Inner Study, 245
Inseparable Souls, 281
Instructions, 235
Insufficient Understanding, 259
Intense Sparks, 94
Interest From G-d, 203
Interface, 169
Isometrics, 114

Jacob's Path, 166
Jealous Angels, 86
Joseph, 71
Joy, 144
Joy Unleashed, 100
Joyful Prognostics, 101
Just a Favor, 39

Keep Going, 111

Landing, 119
Laser Power, 63
Leaving Egypt, 148
Lend on Me, 211
Liberated by Betrothal, 157
Life on Mars, 271
Life That Works, 266
Light Power, 201
Light Unsheathed, 31
Living Jews, 279
Lofty Living, 79

Many Children, 226
Marital Blessing, 222
Marital Peace, 222
Marital Strife, 220
Marriage as Microcosm, 219
Matching Worlds, 76
Medical License, 134
Meditation, 245
Mentors, 128
Metaphor, 66
Microhealing, 25
Mighty Waters, 74

Mindfull, 102
Miracles & Doctors, 132
Miracles Today, 53
Mirrors, 196
Mockery, 89
Momentous Missions, 57
More Light, 33
More Than Stories, 240
Morning Meditation, 246
Mountain Climbing, 202
Multiple Reflections, 236
Mystical & Practical, 240

Never Distant, 281
Noah & Abraham, 151
Not and Is, 47
Not Doing, 189
Not If, But How, 118
Not Making a Living, 70
Not the Body, 91
Nothing to Fear, 285
Nothingness, 160
Now, 35
Nuclear Lessons, 56

Objective Faith, 263
Omniscience and Free Choice, 257
On Computers, 60
On the Third Day There Was Peace, 27
One Candle at a Time, 61
One Last Adjustment, 285
Open Eyes, 292
Out of Center, 103
Owning Wisdom, 246

Parental Behavior, 225
Parental Guidance, 217
Peace at Home, 219
Peek-A-Boo, 48
Penetrating Wisdom, 236
Perceptive Repair, 39
Phase Two, 191
Post-Sinai, 239

Power Talk, 194
Powerful Beauty, 200
Priorities, 82
Prisoners, 146
Proof, 268
Punishment, 224

Questioning the Divine, 261
Questions, 243

Rather Be Praying, 81
Real Ideas, 247
Recognition, 47
Refilling the Void, 31
Resilience, 124
Retroactive Liberation, 290
Return Beyond Time, 126
Return to One, 27
Roles, 215
Running Away, 38

Science & G-d, 270
Science From the Top Down, 273
Scientific Revolution, 272
Seeing Within, 22
Self-Confidence, 105
Self-Destruction, 98
Self-Surrender, 138
Self-Trial, 182
Serious Darkness, 113
Silence Before the Flood, 289
Simple & Earnest, 176
Simple Path, 100
Sincerity, 156
Slaves of Stuff, 82
Small & Infinite, 160
Small Things, 139
Small Truths, 164
Smaller, 159
Smarter, A Little, 258
Soul Healing, 130
Special Soldiers, 197
Spiritual Career, 81
Spontaneous, 190

Spring, 287
Start Simple, 241
Stay Calm, 77
Stay Put, 32
Stereo Lighting, 50
Stereo-Miracles, 51
Subliminal Surrender, 140
Sun & Moon, 248
Sun & Moon II, 249
Sunglasses, 65
Switch on the Light, 127

Tailored to Business, 70
Teacher, 249
Thank You, 198
The Ark, 73
The Astronaut, 58
The Bridge, 22
The Child, 172
The Choice, 83
The Female Home, 216
The Gateway, 145
The Harder Easier Path, 168
The Highest, 145
The Inexplicable, 54
The Infinite Connection, 108
The Journey Home, 179
The Master's Prayer, 276
The Moment, 37
The Most Wondrous, 52
The New Self-Sacrifice, 137
The Other's World, 170
The Rainbow, 122
The Rock, 93
The Rope, 158
The Sewing Needle, 143
The Source, 173
The Sterile Classroom, 230
The Third Path, 167
The Transparent Teacher, 128
The Typist, 84
The Ultimate Sacrifice, 153
Three Loves, 277
Three Possibilities, 169
Time Line, 284

Time Out, 267
Toil, 75
Tolerance, 192
True Belief, 253
True Love, 185
Trust for Others, 187
Two Are One, 264
Two Masters, 216
Two Ones, 185
Two Paths, 166

Ultimate Knowledge, 256
Uncharity, 204
Unconditional Love, 220
Uncovered and Shining, 196
Under Guard, 162
Understanding Wonder, 255
Unfinished Business, 218
Unlimited Channels, 68
Unpraying, 204
Unrepenting, 205
Unsecular Jews, 278

Unveiling the Spark, 78
Us, 21

Wanton Love, 190
Warning, 230
We Are One, 280
Wellsprings, 291
Where Lives the Torah, 237
Where Will I Be?, 287
Which is Greater, 186
Who Owns Truth, 174
Who Will Win, 75
Wisdom & the Rebel, 242
With the Body, 90
Without Measure, 202
Wonder, 241
Words From the Heart, 193
World Defined, 43

Your Jerusalem, 38
Your Will, 158

About the Author

Rabbi Tzvi Freeman is a senior editor at Chabad.org.

About the Rebbe

Rebbe means teacher. **Rabbi Menachem M. Schneerson** took the position of seventh in a prestigious line of Rebbes. Even after his passing, he is known worldwide as simply "The Rebbe"—a Rebbe for any person in the world.

From the time the Rebbe came to America in 1941, people of all faiths and walks of life travelled from afar to seek his advice and hear his wisdom. Politicians, civil rights activists, writers, scientists, religious leaders, scholars, business people, and any person who sought wisdom and guidance, lined up at his door for many hours every week. Sacks of mail arrived daily with requests for guidance and blessings from every corner of the world. His students compiled over forty volumes of his talks, which he edited and annotated.

In 1983, on his 80th birthday, U.S. Congress proclaimed Rabbi Schneerson's birthday, "Education Day, USA," and awarded the Rebbe the National Scroll of Honor.

In 1995, the Rebbe was posthumously awarded the Congressional Gold Medal, an award granted only 130 Americans since Thomas Jefferson, for "outstanding and lasting contributions."

This book offers every person a taste of the Rebbe, condensed from over 50 years of letters, public talks, private conversations and written works, presented in an accessible format.

Printed in Great Britain
by Amazon